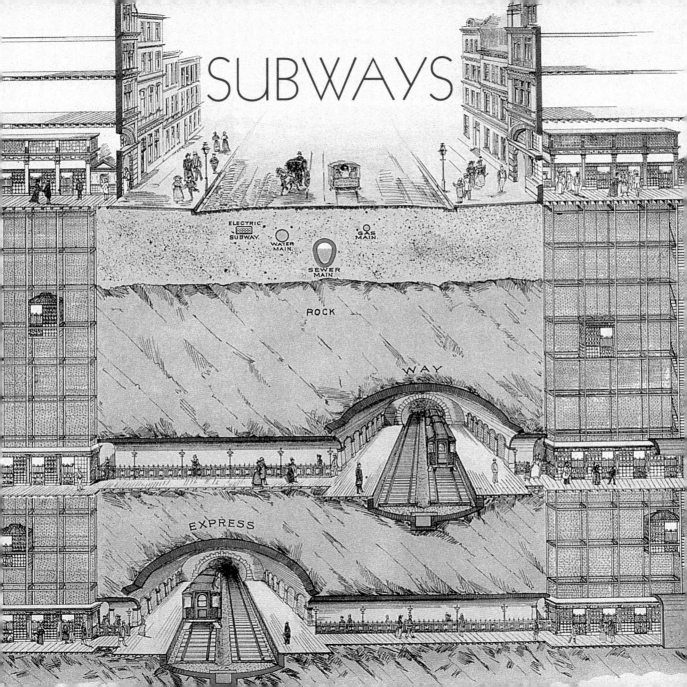

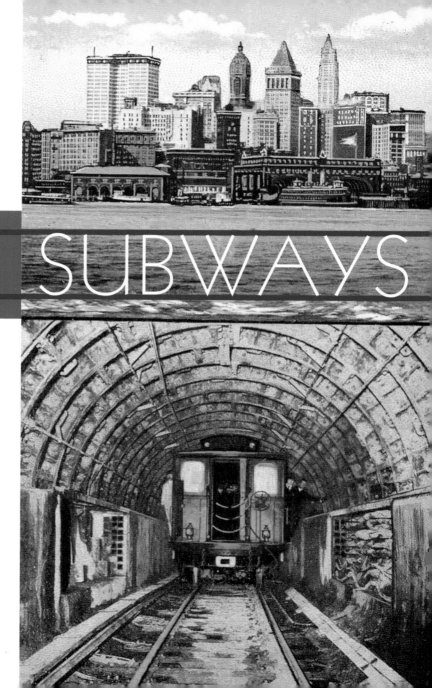

SUBWAYS

Lorraine B. Diehl

CLARKSON POTTER/PUBLISHERS
NEW YORK

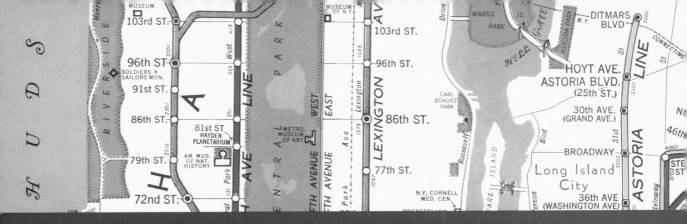

THE TRACKS THAT BUILT NEW YORK CITY

OPPOSITE: A Redbird delivers baseball fans to Yankee Stadium. Collection of Andrew Grahl.

PHOTOGRAPHS ON PAGES 6–7, FROM LEFT TO RIGHT: Sightseers in turn-of-the-century New York City enjoying an open horseless carriage ride. From the author's collection. Early subway maps included the el locations where passengers could transfer to subways. From the author's collection. Much of the beautiful Heins & LaFarge tile work and mosaics still adorn the now abandoned City Hall Station. From the collection of Andrew Grahl. Postcard showing passengers about to board one of the first subway cars in the new City Hall Station, circa 1904. From the author's collection. This mermaid luring straphangers to Coney Island graces a SUBWAY SUN poster, part of a transit system advertising campaign introduced in subway cars in the 1910s. Courtesy of A. Sumner-Sackett. Until 1940, this BMT logo tile could be found at the entrances to all BMT stations. From the collection of Steven Zabel, courtesy of Eric Oszustowicz. The subway token was introduced on July 25, 1953. Courtesy of A. Sumner-Sackett. A ticket chopper in front of his machine. From the Brooklyn Public Library—Brooklyn Collection.

Grateful acknowledgment is made to the following for permission to reprint previously published material: **Cherry Lane Music Publishing Company, Inc.**: "Take the 'A' Train," words and music by Billy Strayhorn. Copyright © 1941; renewed 1969 DreamWorks Songs (ASCAP) and Billy Strayhorn Songs, Inc. (ASCAP) for the U.S.A. Rights for DreamWorks Songs and Billy Strayhorn Songs, Inc. administered by Cherry Lane Music Publishing Company, Inc. International copyright secured. All rights reserved.

Copyright © 2004 by Lorraine B. Diehl

All rights reserved. No part of this book may be reproduced or transmitted in any form or by any means, electronic or mechanical, including photocopying, recording, or by any information storage and retrieval system, without permission in writing from the publisher.

Published by Clarkson Potter/Publishers, New York, New York. Member of the Crown Publishing Group, a division of Random House, Inc.

www.crownpublishing.com

CLARKSON N. POTTER is a trademark and POTTER and colophon are registered trademarks of Random House, Inc.

Printed in Singapore

Design by Jane Treuhaft

Library of Congress Cataloging-in-Publication Data
Diehl, Lorraine B.
    Subways : the tracks that built New York City / Lorraine B. Diehl.
    Includes index.
    1. Subways—New York (State)—New York.   2. Technology—Social aspects—New York (State)—New York.   3. New York (N.Y.)—History.   I. Title.
TF847.N5D54   2004
388.4'28'097471—dc22   2003026130

ISBN 1-4000-5227-0

10 9 8 7 6 5 4 3 2 1

First Edition

For Dom and for Ellie

PROLOGUE 8

IT'S WORTH YOUR LIFE TO CROSS BROADWAY! 16

"TO HARLEM IN FIFTEEN MINUTES!" 28

THAT ELEGANT, SWELL-EGANT SUBWAY RIDE 38

HEY! WHAT ABOUT BROOKLYN? 48

FROM ORCHARD STREET TO GREEN PASTURES 58

THE AVENUES OF EXPANSION 68

CONTENTS

NEW YORK'S LOVE-HATE RELATIONSHIP WITH THE THIRD AVENUE EL 80

NEW YORK'S TROLLEY SONG 88

SUBWAY STOPS ALONG THE WAY 96

TAKE ME OUT TO THE BALLGAME! 106

THE RISE AND FALL AND RISE AGAIN OF THE SUBWAY 116

EPILOGUE 124   ACKNOWLEDGMENTS 125

SOURCES 126   BIBLIOGRAPHY 127   INDEX 128

PROLOGUE

It was an astounding idea. The notion that one could walk into a marble building on the southwest corner of Warren Street and Broadway, which housed Devlin's Clothing Store, and descend to the store's basement into an elegant salon equipped with a grand piano, a decorative water fountain, a goldfish tank, and walls hung with oil paintings was the stuff of dreams. Passing through the salon, one descended six steps and approached twin bronze statues of Mercury—the mythic God of speed—each bearing a cluster of red, white, and blue gaslights, before boarding a circular wooden car. The car had oiled wooden floors and glowed from the light of a single zircon lamp. Taking a seat on one of the two richly upholstered couches, one waited as the single door closed. The car was then pushed through a tunnel the length of a city block from Warren to Murray Street, and drawn back again at a speed of ten miles an hour. There were no horses pulling the car. It was propelled by a giant fan near the Warren Street entrance, which blew the car toward Murray Street, "like a sailboat before the wind." At Murray Street the car would trip a wire, which rang a bell back at Warren Street, alerting the engineer to reverse the great fan. The wooden car would then be sucked back to Warren Street, where passengers would disembark, climb the stairs to Devlin's Clothing Store, and exit into nineteenth-century New York City. What is even more astounding about this block-long subway line that opened its door to New Yorkers in 1870 is the fact that it was built in secret.

Alfred Ely Beach was a brilliant man—journalist, patent lawyer, and inventor—born with a restless mind and a fertile imagination. At twenty, while a student at Yale, he borrowed money to buy a fledgling magazine called *Scientific American* and transformed it into the popular journal of science it remains today. By the age of thirty, he had invented and patented a typewriter for the blind, which was awarded first prize and a gold medal at New York's Crystal Palace Exhibition. But in 1868 the forty-two-year-old Beach—who was now publishing both *Scientific American* and his father's newspaper, the *New York Sun*—looked out his office window near City Hall onto the traffic-clogged streets of Broadway and decided the time had come to demonstrate one of his most dynamic inventions.

New York City was still in its adolescence in the mid-1860s, and it suffered terribly from the growing pains of urban expansion. Mansions north of Thirty-fourth Street—until now the dividing line between the rich and the rest of the city—were making way for modest row houses; merchant princes, for countinghouse clerks, teachers, and doctors. East Fifty-ninth Street, once an enclave of country estates, now boasted block upon block of brick houses beckoning the middle class. On the West Side William B. Astor constructed two hundred row houses from Forty-fourth to Forty-seventh Street between Ninth Avenue and Broadway. The city grew larger, but still it remained dense, as more and more people called New York home. This was the city that Alfred Ely Beach knew was desperate for better transportation.

Beach had introduced his invention, called the pneumatic tube, at the Fourteenth Street Armory's American Institute Fair in 1867. His air-propelled device was similar to a smaller version invented in England forty years earlier, designed to transport mail through a series of tunnels beneath the streets of London. But Alfred Ely Beach was interested in delivering more than packages. At the fair, Beach displayed two versions of his invention: a small tube, not unlike London's model, to deliver the mail, and a much larger tube—six feet in diameter and one hundred feet long— in which a car holding ten passengers would take them on their first horseless ride. The giant tube, which was suspended from the Armory ceiling by huge iron rings, became the hit of the fair. Day after day, people lined up to ride through Beach's tube, from Fourteenth to Fifteenth Street, in the single car that was powered by an enormous fan. By the time the fair ended, more than seventy-five thousand future straphangers had taken a ride on Beach's pneumatic tube.

In 1868, state senator and notoriously corrupt city leader Boss Tweed decided what would and what would not be built in New York, and the only projects the graft-addicted politician allowed to rise were those that could give him a hefty slice of the pie. Beach wanted to build the city's first subway, but he knew that the man who sat in Tammany Hall, just a shadow's length from the *Sun*'s offices, would have his hand out, and Beach refused to pay him off. "I won't pay political blackmail," he told his brother. "I say, let's build it furtively."

"We propose to run the line to Central Park, about five miles in all," he would eventually proclaim. "When completed, we should be able to carry twenty thousand passengers a day at speeds up to a mile a minute." But for now there were no proclamations, just secret plans. For nineteenth-century New Yorkers, Beach's idea for a subway line was beyond comprehension. No one went down into the earth to get from one part of the city to another.

But Beach was crafty. Realizing that he needed a franchise to tunnel under the streets of Manhattan, Beach submitted a proposal to build two mail tubes, each of them four and a half feet in diameter, which would deliver mail under Broadway between Warren and Cedar streets. The proximity of the proposed tubes to the new post office being built just south of City Hall could only enhance the prospects for Beach's project in the eyes of Tammany's "Grand Sachem." Not surprisingly, Tweed gave Beach his stamp of approval and issued the charter. Then while Tweed's sights were set on other profit-making ventures, Beach went back to the legislature and asked for an amendment to build one large tube instead of two small ones. To save money and simplify construction, Beach argued. No problem, he was told. Build your single tunnel.

Beach must have been walking on air. Not only had he gotten the green light to build his subway tunnel, but it would be built under the blind eye of the politician

PHOTOGRAPH ON PAGE 8: Original ticket of admission issued by Beach's Pneumatic Transit Company for the one-block subway ride. Courtesy of Lawrence Stelter.

OPPOSITE: Passengers test Beach's pneumatic tube at the 1867 American Institute Fair. Museum of the City of New York.

OPPOSITE TOP: The "Western Tornado" propels Beach's secret subway beneath Warren Street. Museum of the City of New York.

OPPOSITE BOTTOM: Passengers riding in comfort in the elegant pneumatic car. Museum of the City of New York.

he had just managed to outfox. Now, Beach knew that he couldn't burrow under the streets of Manhattan for something as ambitious as a subway tunnel without someone noticing, so he decided to build a prototype—a subway line, with one hidden station, that actually went nowhere—figuring that once New Yorkers fell in love with the idea, Tweed would be powerless to stop the real thing. And, to make sure the meddling Tweed didn't get suspicious, Beach would dig out his tunnel at night.

Each evening when most New Yorkers were asleep, Beach's twenty-one-year-old son, Frederic, whom Alfred had made foreman, met with his eight-man crew in the basement of Devlin's Clothing Store and began excavating the shallow subbasement. None of these men had ever been inside a tunnel, and apprehension ran high at the notion of digging belowground through the dark and dankness into the unknown, with nothing but candlelight for illumination. They had not counted on the stench and the heat, nor the din of Broadway traffic above them, which was amplified in the hollow work space, setting their nerves on edge. They were 21½ feet below Broadway when they shoveled the first spadefuls of excavated dirt into a corner of Devlin's basement. Once the tunnel work was ready to begin, Alfred Beach employed another of his inventions: the Beach Tunneling Shield, a giant iron cylinder designed to work more efficiently than the one used for London's Underground, which had been completed in 1863. Beach's shield, which was driven forward by hydraulic jacks, could push into the earth at the rate of eight feet each night while the men carried the excavated dirt in wagons with wheels muffled for silence to the edge of the city. "Night after night," wrote Robert Daley in *The World Beneath the City*, "gangs of men slipped in and out of the tunnel like thieves." Others arrived to brick up the new tunnel. At one point, when they hit a stone wall that was thought to have been the remains of an old fort, Beach ordered the men to dismantle it stone by stone. For fifty-eight nights, men dug and hauled and bricked until Beach's subway tunnel was finished.

The single subway car was built so that it fit perfectly into the nine-foot cylindrical tube. The elegant waiting room, measuring more than a third of the entire 312-foot tunnel, was finished. Next, the grand piano, the decorative fountain, and the goldfish tank were installed. Lastly came the great fan that would put everything in motion. It was officially known as the Roots Patent Force Blast Blower, but everyone who worked in the tunnel called it "the Western Tornado." The fifty-ton fan, which was placed near the Warren Street waiting room, was operated by a steam engine, drawing air in through a valve and blowing it into the tunnel at the rate of one hundred thousand cubic feet a minute.

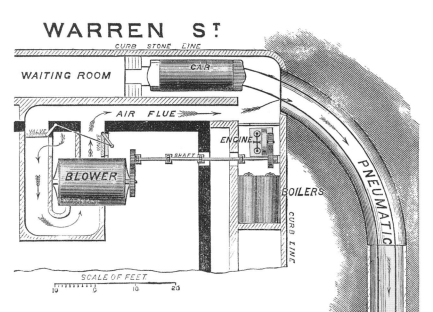

On February 26, 1870, two years and $350,000 later, Alfred Ely Beach uncovered his secret, and New Yorkers woke up to discover that they had a subway. An "Aladdin's cave" wrote a *New York Herald* reporter, one of several members of the press who were invited, along with state and city officials, to the "Under Broadway Reception" hosted by Beach. A *New York Times* reporter noted how surprised everyone was to find not "a dismal cavernous retreat," but an "elegant reception room, the light, airy tunnel, and the general appearance of taste and comfort in all the apartments." Beach decided on the opulent waiting room with its grand piano and bubbling fountain to allay the apprehension of first-time passengers who might balk at traveling below the city streets. He would simply seduce them with grandeur. New Yorkers loved it. During the first year of

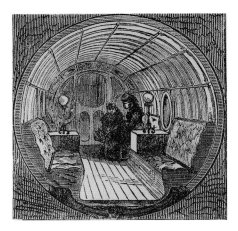

operation, they descended into Devlin's Clothing Store basement at the rate of more than a thousand passengers a day, parting with twenty-five cents—a substantial sum at the time—for the privilege.

For three years, Beach's pneumatic subway car blew back and forth between Warren and Murray streets, charming New Yorkers with the ride to nowhere. But in 1873 the subway took its last ride, and the enterprise was closed down. It wasn't because of Tweed, whose popularity and power, by then, had finally begun to wither after a series of scathing *New York Times* articles exposed his dirty dealings. Beach's novelty ride had simply worn thin. In truth, pneumatic propulsion was no way to run a subway. Even Beach saw that. In 1873 the state legislature in Albany had actually given Beach the green light for his subway, overruling the objections of the mighty John Jacob Astor, who feared that a tunnel under Broadway would send the 280-foot spire of Trinity Church crashing to the ground. In the end, compressed air proved to be too costly and inflexible for running a network of trains. It worked fine for the mail. From 1897 right into 1953, New York City's post office had a twenty-seven-mile pneumatic mail system with "rockateers" sending mail-filled canisters through a network of underground tubes. Mail was literally blown around the city, from the General Post Office to Manhattanville, Times Square, Radio City Music Hall, and other post offices throughout Manhattan.

Beach ended up renting out his subway tunnel as a wine cellar, a shooting gallery, and a storage vault. His pneumatic subway had cost him greatly. It had depleted his fortune and exhausted his spirit, and on New Year's Day in 1896, at sixty-nine, he was dead. Two years later, on a cold December day, a raging fire destroyed Devlin's Clothing Store, giving New Yorkers an opportunity to walk through the charred debris and descend once more into Beach's dream tunnel to see what remained. They poked around, looking in the dust and dirt for remnants of the vanished waiting room. Someone took a photograph of a man sitting in the shell of the rotted subway car.

By 1912, when the city made plans for the new Brooklyn Rapid Transit line (later to be called the

BMT) to tunnel under Broadway for its City Hall station, they hired the Degnon Contracting Company to excavate and build their tunnel. On February 8, several of their engineers, together with a handful of reporters and city officials, went down into Beach's old tunnel to see just what was left. Since it had been sealed over years before, they entered through the ventilating shaft, across from Murray Street, just inside City Hall Park. In the darkness, they could make out Beach's shield still pressed against the tunnel's end at Murray Street. Remarkably, the tunnel was very much intact, its iron rings still solid. Although Beach's wooden car had mostly rotted away, some remnants of it remained. Beach's shield was removed and given to his son Frederic, who sent it to Cornell University. It was put on exhibition but then disappeared.

There is a postscript, an amusing one that would likely make Alfred Ely Beach smile: In a scene from *Ghostbusters II*, Dan Aykroyd comes upon an underground tunnel bearing the name Pneumatic Transit System, through which slithers the film's familiar ectoplasmic slime. "I can't believe it!" gasps Aykroyd as the famous ghostbuster. "It's still here!"

OPPOSITE: Beach's elegant subway entrance assured New Yorkers that it was safe to travel below the city's streets. Museum of the City of New York.

LEFT: Beach's subway car departing from Warren Street. Museum of the City of New York.

IT'S WORTH YOUR LIFE

In 1866 a haberdasher named John Genin offered to buy a bridge. Not the Brooklyn Bridge—that hadn't been built yet—but one that would arch across Broadway just below St. Paul's Chapel at Fulton Street, where his store was located. Genin was so desperate to get his customers over to the east side of the street where his hat shop was that he was willing to underwrite the cost of a pedestrian bridge. Genin's bridge wasn't built, but another ornate iron one known as the Loew Bridge rose on the spot and stood there for two years.

With the Civil War over, New York City, already the largest city in the Western hemisphere, was more prosperous than ever. Its ports were humming, and manufacturing was up and running. Everything from books to sugar to clothing was being produced on a massive scale on the narrow island of Manhattan. Along the East River, over a thousand men working for the Novelty Iron Works made the machinery that ran the city's many factories. Wall Street was bustling as gambling

TO CROSS BROADWAY!

fever gripped the market. Newspapers like the *New York World*, the *Sun* and the *New York Tribune*—three of more than a dozen dailies—were spinning off the presses along Park Row's "Newspaper Row." Almost weekly, new restaurants popped up to accommodate businessmen rushing out for lunch.

Light industry was establishing itself just outside of the city in Brooklyn and Newark, New Jersey, but not on the scale of Manhattan, which had close to five thousand "shops" producing umbrellas, shoes, jewelry, and countless other items for consumption. Filling these jobs were the endless streams of immigrants landing daily at Castle Garden, the processing center that had been set up in 1855 at the southern tip of Manhattan. By 1860, of the more than eight hundred thousand people living on the island of Manhattan, nearly half of those were immigrants. They were joined each morning by young men from Brooklyn and New Jersey who ferried across the rivers to their jobs in the city. Every corner of downtown Manhattan was alive with activity. If this wasn't enough to clog the streets, upper- and middle-class women came to shop in the department stores rising along lower Broadway. And some made the trip to work there. One emporium, A. T. Stewart's "Cast-Iron Palace" on Broadway, between Ninth and Tenth streets, employed hundreds of seamstresses in catering to the carriage trade. This prosperous, energetic New York City was also attracting tourists who were filling the new hotels.

Because more than half of New York worked and lived below Fourteenth Street, this narrow strip of real estate is where most of the traffic congregated. Omnibuses, horsecars, hansom cabs, carriages, and drays raced up and down eighty-foot-wide Broadway, all unfettered by traffic lights. Pedestrians didn't stand a chance. "At Broadway near Trinity Church the clutter of the buses and carriages made travel a constant adventure of narrow escapes and near accidents," wrote Robert C. Reed in *The New*

PREVIOUS PAGES: A typical 1855 traffic jam on lower Broadway in front of Barnum's Museum. Museum of the City of New York.

OPPOSITE: The ferryboat JOHN G. MCCULLOUGH bound for Manhattan, 1896. Museum of the City of New York, the Byron Collection.

LEFT: Horsecars, omni-buses, and drays push along a very congested Broadway in this 1883 wood engraving. Museum of the City of New York.

● ABOVE: This 1848 illustration shows one of several proposals for a street railroad to alleviate traffic along narrow Broadway. Museum of the City of New York.

York Elevated. In the year the Loew Bridge went up, New York City had twenty-nine omnibus and fourteen horsecar lines carrying one hundred million passengers daily. The city also had its own horse railway—the first in the world—inaugurated on November 26, 1832, by the New York & Harlem Railroad, running along the Bowery from Prince to Fourteenth Street.

Aiding and abetting the traffic mess were the ferries spewing commuters from Brooklyn, Staten Island, and New Jersey onto the city's narrow toe. Then there was the New York & Harlem Railroad's steam line chugging down the spine of the island from Harlem to City Hall, fouling the air with soot until it reached Twenty-seventh Street, where the locomotive was forced by city ordinance to switch to real horsepower.

Exacerbating the impossible congestion was the horrendous condition of the streets. Gaping holes from loosened cobblestones quickly filled with rotting garbage

■ RIGHT: The last horsecar to operate in New York City was the South Ferry to Central Park Line (circa 1910). Fiorello H. LaGuardia Collection: La Guardia & Wagner Archives.

and fetid slush as inadequate sewers clogged and broke. Tons of manure from the tens of thousands of over-worked horses fell onto the streets, which remained slippery as glass from the constant rain of horse urine.

If it was nearly impossible for pedestrians to dodge traffic, passengers riding the omnibuses and horsecars didn't fare much better. The brightly colored

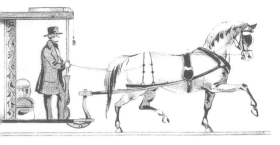

omnibuses, with their delicate, salon-quality paintings etched on their sides, might have had a certain visual charm, but riding in these overgrown stagecoaches—holdovers from the 1820s—was, according to James D. McCabe, Jr., in *Lights and Shadows of New York Life* "as rough as [riding in] an old-fashioned country wagon." Since omnibuses were only meant to seat fifteen, passengers cramped for space rode on the roof, their legs dangling down in Wild West–fashion and their bones and teeth rattling as the omnibus lumbered along the bumpy road.

Ironically, these coaches were considered a more genteel mode of transportation than the more contemporary horsecars, which rode along embedded iron tracks, providing a smoother ride. They were larger and cheaper than the buses, with access to the northernmost reaches of the city. They were also dirty and overcrowded, with eighty or more passengers packed into a car designed for twenty-two. With the scents of perspiration, and the garbage-filled streets mingling in one odiferous bouquet, the passenger was cautioned to "lose his sense of smell [and] have the capacity to shut himself up like a patent umbrella." Even attempts to make riders comfortable backfired. During the winter months, mice infested the straw laid down for warmth. And neither mode of transportation got you anywhere fast. "We can travel from New York half-way to Philadelphia in less time than the length of Broadway," commented the *New York Tribune*.

Nowhere has necessity prodded invention more urgently than on the streets of New York City in the late 1860s. Schemes to get people around town faster had been popping up everywhere, vying with Alfred Beach's dream subway long before he ordered his waiting-room furniture. While Beach went underground, others made their plans in the air. In the 1850s, designs for elevated systems appeared almost weekly in newspapers and magazines. According to Robert Reed in *The New York Elevated*, "companies sprang up in second-floor offices along Broadway, each with a patent, a prospectus, and a collection of testimonials." Even Beach's *Scientific American* published the plans of several el designers.

Alfred Speer of Passaic, New Jersey, came up with the idea of a giant loop—a kind of continuously moving conveyor belt circling the city—on which people could ride, walk, or rest in any number of salons until they came to their destination. In 1872 Dr. Rufus Gilbert, a former Civil War army surgeon, took Beach's idea of pneumatic propulsion and brought it aboveground. Gilbert envisioned one long Gothic arch straddling Broadway with dual tubes through which circular streetcars would be

propelled. Another elevated, this one proposed by J. B. Wickersham, called for a horse railway above the sidewalk with a companion pedestrian promenade nearly touching nearby buildings. Although thieves and voyeurs may have delighted at such a prospect, those who lived in the buildings along the routes had to be horrified.

While schemes for an elevated railway floated about the city, Charles T. Harvey, a Connecticut inventor, actually began building one, not on Broadway, but on nearby Greenwich Street, away from the glare of sabotaging politicians whose interests in horsecar lines discouraged overhead competition. Actually, Harvey won approval to build his ambitious West Side and Yonkers Patent Railway from the state legislature in 1867 because it would be built off the beaten track. He also promised to erect a quarter mile of test track and to take it down at his own expense if it failed. Nicknamed the "one-legged railway" because of the single slender track running above the sidewalk, supported by thirty-foot-high columns, Harvey's iron creature stirred up mighty dreams for the inventor. He envisioned a twenty-five-mile track stretching from the Battery to the wilds of Yonkers. A second East Side line would run up Third Avenue, crossing the Harlem River until it reached New Rochelle more than twenty miles away. Since New York City's heavily developed area just about ended at Forty-second Street, this was one ambitious project.

Harvey was given a one-year deadline to construct something before the state legislature agreed to give him a final green light. He didn't need the year. On a cold

Sunday morning in December 1867, Charles Harvey made a special trial run just for supporters of his elevated, taking a quarter-mile ride from the Battery to Morris Street, riding high above the gawking spectators in his specially built handcar: a glorified go-cart with giant metal wheels. The movers and shakers liked what they saw and told Harvey to forge ahead.

ABOVE: Inventor Charles Harvey in a hand-car testing his cable-operated elevated railway, December 7, 1867. Museum of the City of New York.

His elevated railway—the first in the world—was operated by cables powered by steam engines, much like the cable cars in San Francisco. A three-quarter-inch steel cable manufactured by John Roebling, who would soon design the Brooklyn Bridge, ran continuously underground. Drivers would clamp on to the moving cable that ran through the bottom of the cars to get them moving. Four cable-operating plants kept the cables in motion. There would be only three cars running back and forth on a single track, with occasional side rails to allow for passing cars.

By 1869, the first segment of the Greenwich Street elevated, as New Yorkers would soon call it, stretched north to Twenty-ninth Street and Ninth Avenue. Harvey needed to link his elevated with the Hudson River Railroad depot at Thirtieth Street—just a short distance away—giving passengers a vital connection to the suburbs if he was to make a profit. But competing horsecar interests threatened to tie him up in time-consuming litigation. Then on September 24, "Black Friday," a devastating bank panic swept the country, and Harvey and his $200,000 of working capital for the railway were sucked into the whirlpool of financial loss. Desperate for funds to finance the Thirtieth Street link, he entered into a Faustian pact with a group of unscrupulous bankers who kept his elevated afloat with a loan but then promptly took it over. Without Charles Harvey's vision and enthusiasm the company foundered, the tracks rusted, and on November 15, 1870, everything that was once part of the West Side and Yonkers Railway was sold off at a sheriff's auction for the grand price of $960.

OPPOSITE TOP: Alfred Speer's proposal for an elevated walkway with a continuously moving platform. OPPOSITE BOTTOM, Dr. Rufus Gilbert's ornate Gothic arches, which would have encased air-propelled cars as part of his 1872 elevated railway. Both images from Museum of the City of New York.

OPPOSITE: The luxury of the Gilbert elevated Pullman car was a far cry from overcrowded horsecars. Museum of the City of New York.

BELOW: As New York pushed uptown at the turn of the twentieth century, the area north of Forty-second Street was still largely undeveloped. Here, trolleys pass Grand Central Depot in 1900 (LEFT). From the author's collection. By then, subway construction was planned but not yet begun in Columbus Circle (CENTER). Print by Trolleyworks@AOL.com, courtesy of Joseph P. Saitta. In 1878, a year later the American Museum of Natural History opened, it still sat in swampland (RIGHT). American Museum of Natural History Library.

A year later, a phoenix rose from the rubble of Harvey's dream: the New York Elevated Railway, which would eventually become part of a 160-mile network of lines that, like Harvey's "one-legged railway," would deliver New Yorkers to northern Westchester. The New York Elevated Railway got rid of underground cables and put steam locomotives in front of their cars. And there now would be not one but two tracks as it made its way up the island of Manhattan via Ninth Avenue. By the summer of 1873, the elevated arrived at Thirty-fourth Street and Ninth Avenue, and by 1875 it had reached Forty-second Street.

A year later it delivered passengers to Sixty-first Street and Columbus Avenue, a stop that was singularly responsible for the emergence of Manhattan's thriving Upper West Side. Before the arrival of the el, the only public transportation to this neighborhood was the cumbersome Eighth Avenue horsecar, which required a change at Fifty-ninth Street, or the Hudson River Railroad, making local stops along the river. In the 1870s the Upper West Side of Manhattan was a strange hodgepodge of deteriorating country mansions, colonies of squatters living in rows of hovels, and the promise of a revitalized community. Anticipating the city's push northward, the old Bloomingdale Road running up the area's spine was rebuilt with elm trees shading it in the style of a European boulevard. What residents knew as "the Boulevard" would eventually become upper Broadway. A strip of waterfront running parallel to the Hudson River had been acquired for Riverside Park and by

1885 the new park stretched as far north as 145th Street. But streets were slow in getting paved; the area around the new American Museum of Natural History was still mostly swampland when the museum opened in 1877. By the time the el reached 104th Street, brownstones were rising in the blocks along its stops, and apartment houses for the new middle class, with stores on the ground level, began to dot the avenues.

In 1875, the year the elevated reached Forty-second Street, New York City got its first Rapid Transit Commission, which would decide what kind of public transportation would be built and what routes that transportation would take. The commission also decided what kind of power would drive all public transportation. Remember Dr. Rufus Gilbert, the army surgeon whose Gothic-arched railway was supposed to shoot trains through pneumatic tubes? Because the city had given him a franchise to build his Wellesian-like contraption a few years before—one that included some very desirable routes—the Gilbert elevated was finally attracting investors. Gilbert was told to deep-six his notion of pneu-matically powered trains and accept steam-powered locomotives. He also had to abandon those Gothic arches. Unfortunately, the financially naïve Gilbert made the same unwitting bargain as had Charles Harvey, and the inventor woke up one morning to find that his stock had been sold out from under him. Nevertheless, the elevated would bear his name . . . if only temporarily.

On June 5, 1878, the Gilbert elevated was finally in operation; its handsome apple-green Pullman cars with leather seats were ready to carry New Yorkers up Sixth Avenue from South Ferry all the way north to Central Park. And to add a bit of icing to this tasty cake, the first day's ride was free. The spacious cars accommodated fifty seated passengers. Gone was the mice-ridden straw of the horsecars. Steam pipes placed beneath the seats would ward off the winter's chill. To attract all strata of society, first-class cars were available for ten cents (double the regular fare). First-class passengers

walked on colorful Axminster carpets and took their seats amidst oak and mahogany walls painted with murals. Tapestry curtains blocked the sun's glare, and at night, light was provided by oil-lamp chandeliers. Newspapers lavished praise upon the new line. The *New York Herald* wrote: "The ladies were evidently charmed with its spacious and elegant coaches, decorated with all the taste and finish of a boudoir." The paper went on to describe the ride as "exhilarating to the spirits and gratifying to the mind." A few days later, all traces of the man who started the line vanished when Gilbert's name was removed from his elevated and it was renamed the Metropolitan Railway.

A year later, on September 1, 1879, the Metropolitan Railway and the New York Elevated merged and became known as the Manhattan Elevated Company. By year's end, the Manhattan West Side els reached as far north as 155th Street; the East Side els, 129th Street. Eighty-one miles of elevated track now ran up and down Manhattan, winding around the serpentine curve of the Lower East Side's Coenties Slip and stretching high over the daunting Suicide Curve at 110th Street. They would soon carry 14 million New Yorkers from the island's tip into the woodlands of the Bronx. The els were changing the face of the city, cutting swaths of new urban landscape with their tracks.

Then, just two years before the arrival of the twentieth century, that landscape broadened dramatically as the people living in the bucolic enclaves of Brooklyn, Queens, Staten Island, and the Bronx joined with Manhattanites to become citizens of Greater New York. For thirty years Andrew Haskell Green, the city comptroller, had dreamed of bringing together the areas surrounding Manhattan and creating one imperial city divided into five boroughs. At the time, Queens and Staten Island were mostly farmland, while Brooklyn, a former village, was becoming a thriving city, incorporating the other four towns the Dutch had laid out in the original settlement of 1636. By 1874 parts of the western Bronx were already annexed to Manhattan, and with the Manhattan Elevated reaching north as far as 110th Street, more of Westchester County would soon become part of New York City. Separated from Manhattan by nothing more than the slender East and Harlem rivers and by

New York Bay, it seemed to Green that nature had conspired to join these interdependent areas into one great metropolis.

Public transportation was the final push behind consolidation. Ferries had always delivered commuters from Brooklyn into Manhattan. Then, with the opening of the Brooklyn Bridge in 1883, the Brooklyn Elevated Railroad was born, eventually delivering more passengers to the city. Two more bridges spanning the East River would follow. Beyond the bridges, talk of tunnels burrowing beneath the river was very much in the air. Not only would commuters living in other boroughs come into the city, but those pressed into overcrowded neighborhoods would be able to spread out beyond Manhattan's shoreline.

At the stroke of midnight, on January 1, 1898, one hundred thousand New Yorkers, who had gathered on the snow-covered lawns of City Hall, waited as Mayor James Phelan of San Francisco, 3,250 miles away, pressed a button igniting an electric impulse that raised the new blue-and-white flag of Greater New York atop City Hall's cupola. Fireworks burst overhead as a one-hundred-gun salute pierced the night air. At that moment, New York City became the largest city in the country, with a population of nearly 3.5 million. Of that number, 1.74 million New Yorkers would ride the els, standing cheek by jowl in overcrowded cars as they had half a century earlier in those horse-drawn cars and buses.

The Empire City had arrived, drawing more people to its streets and its elevateds. Although the days of John Genin's bridge were long gone, the need to move great numbers of people around the city quickly and safely was still paramount. New Yorkers were about to discover that with traffic still clogging their streets and the elevateds rumbling above, there was nowhere to go but down.

OPPOSITE: "Suicide Curve" rose 100 feet above street traffic in Morningside Heights and served the Sixth and Ninth Avenue els. Museum of the City of New York.

THE GRAND DISPLAY OF FIREWORKS AND ILLUMINATIONS

LEFT: The opening of the Brooklyn Bridge on May 24, 1883. © Bettman/CORBIS.

HOTEL
NORMANDIE
ABSOLUTELY
FIRE PROOF

"TO HARLEM

The main object of the road was to carry to and from their homes in the upper portions of Manhattan Island the great army of workers who spend the business day in the offices, shops, and warehouses of the lower portions.

THE NEW YORK SUBWAY:
ITS CONSTRUCTION AND EQUIPMENT
Interborough Rapid Transit, 1904

New Yorkers could barely contain themselves. For months they had been reading about cars that would whisk along underground tracks from lower Manhattan all the way up to the Bronx Zoo. Fifteen minutes, they had heard. Fifteen minutes from City Hall to Harlem. In 1900, with the subway still four long years away, it had to stretch their imaginations to know that they would one day be descending below their sidewalks to board a train, one that would deliver them quickly and efficiently to so many parts of the city. And not a moment too soon.

At the turn of the century, Manhattan was experiencing a building boom fueled by a wave of prosperity as it continued its push uptown. The shopping district that had not long ago clustered around Union Square now reached Twenty-third Street, and Fifth Avenue above Forty-second Street was firmly established as Millionaire's Row. Most New Yorkers worked long hours in the shops and factories that fed on the bur-

IN FIFTEEN MINUTES!"

PREVIOUS PAGES: Trolleys and horsecars travel south along Broadway at Herald Square as the Sixth Avenue el approaches Thirty-third Street. Museum of the City of New York.

OPPOSITE: While New Yorkers celebrated the dawn of their own "golden era," other parts of the country were still mired in the turmoil of 19th century America, as witnessed in the Sunday, March 25, 1900 edition of the NEW YORK HERALD. General Research Division, the New York Public Library, Astor, Lenox, and Tilden Foundations.

geoning economy, usually for little money. As immigrants poured into the city, more people were squeezed into tenements. Sidewalks were jammed at all hours, and now electric automobiles were appearing in the streets, adding to the impossible traffic. Clearly, progress was racing ahead of the city's limited space.

Finally, on March 24, Mayor Robert Van Wyck descended the steps of City Hall into the bright spring sunshine and walked to the tiny park nearby. In his right hand was a silver spade made by Tiffany & Co., bearing the imprint of history. Its wooden handle was made from the bark of the thirteen gum trees that were planted in 1803 in Washington Heights by Alexander Hamilton to symbolize the original thirteen states. Its oak grip was once part of Admiral Perry's flagship, *Lawrence*, which had sailed to victory on Lake Erie during the War of 1812. Surrounding the mayor on the park's lawns and spilling into the narrow streets were twenty-five thousand New Yorkers ready to party.

As the first spadeful of earth was tossed into the air, one hundred thousand pounds of dynamite began exploding from the roof of the nearby Pulitzer Building, showering the spectators with fireworks, a gift to New Yorkers from the *New York World*. John Philip Sousa struck up his band, its rousing music joined by factory whistles and church bells and the wails from boats docked along both rivers. A twenty-one-gun-salute was fired and according to the *New York World* who sponsored it, after each volley the now-familiar "To Harlem in Fifteen Minutes!" chant rose from the crowd in an exuberant chorus. According to Benson Bobrick in *Labyrinths of Iron*, "Twenty great 'flag bombs' blasted into flight, each holding in its core 144 tiny American flags of silk." The sky rained flags that afternoon, most of them claimed by New Yorkers as mementos of the day the building of their subway began.

The battle to build a subway had been hard-fought for ten years, with obstacles popping up like potholes along the way. One hurdle was the real-estate industry, worried that the digging would undermine building foundations and make it impossible for customers to shop at their stores. Then there was the ghost of the unforgettable Boss Tweed, whose tainted cloud of corruption still clung to Tammany Hall, darkening any notion of the Rapid Transit Railroad commissioners making the new subway a public enterprise. Instead, they decided to bid out a franchise, and on

SILVER SPADE OPENS THE GOLDEN TRANSIT ERA

JOHN B. McDONALD

MAYOR VAN WYCK USES THE SILVER SPADE.

FARE.

AUGUST BELMONT

ALEXANDER E. ORR

THE MAYOR AND COMMITTEE IN FRONT OF CITY HALL.

TROOPS WITHDRAWN; LYNCHING FOLLOWS

Mob at Emporia, Va., Quickly Strings Up Cotton and O'Grady After Governor Tyler Had Ordered Soldiers Away at the Request of County Officials.

WHITES HANG NEGRO; NEGROES DEMAND DEATH OF WHITE

Former County Judge, Who Had Led First Attack on Jail, Pleaded in Vain for the Life of the Second Victim—Officials Made No Resistance in Either Case.

INITIAL STROKE FOR GREATEST NEW YORK

Most Important Bit of Earth Removed from the Surface of Manhattan Island Since the Turf Was Pierced for

January 16, 1900, John B. MacDonald, an Irish-American from County Cork, won the bid to build the subway. MacDonald had dug a railroad tunnel beneath Park Avenue for Cornelius Vanderbilt, but he also had a close relationship with Tammany Hall where he could act as a buffer between the Irish political machine and the wary Board of Rapid Transit Commissioners. The one thing MacDonald did not have was money, at least not the required $1 million deposit.

Enter August Belmont, wealthy investment banker and agent for the House of Rothschild in London and Paris. The Harvard-bred scion of his father's vast fortune was fascinated with mass transit and its effect on large cities. Belmont, who also had a passion for subways, agreed to build, equip, and operate a subway for New York City. The proposed train line would run for a period of fifty years with

a renewable option for another twenty-five. The city kicked in a construction budget of $35 million, plus another $1.5 million for land and subway stations, but everything else—the cars, equipment, and electric signals—came from the deep pockets of Mr. Belmont. In April 1902, two years after that first spadeful of earth was dug out for the subway, August Belmont formed the Interborough Rapid Transit Company, to be known by future straphangers as the IRT.

The plan was to start the subway at City Hall (even though most of the city's business was still conducted quite a few blocks away at the city's southern tip), then head north by way of Elm Street (now Lafayette Street) and Park Avenue to Grand Central Station where it would turn west to Times Square (then called Longacre Square), then proceed north again along Broadway to Ninety-sixth Street where it would fork, forming a lopsided V. The western prong of the V would travel through Harlem and Washington Heights to Riverdale until it reached Van Cortlandt Park. The eastern prong would travel up Lenox Avenue and Southern Boulevard until it arrived at Bronx Park. This route was known in subway jargon as Contract One.

New Yorkers were euphoric to know that their subway was finally getting under way, but as they watched streets torn up around them, it soon became clear that this would be a sobering process. Because the topography of Manhattan changes dramatically from one end of the island to the other, the method of subway tunneling was site-specific and hardly rote. It had to deal with the flat, sandy ground running from the island's tip to Twenty-third Street, large tracts of which had once been marshland. (In the early days, when the banks of the East and Hudson rivers overflowed, one could row across

the breadth of the island at Canal Street.) Above Twenty-third Street, up to 103rd Street, the island's topography is dominated by the famous Manhattan schist, a hard rock that does not easily yield. Then there is the area above 103rd Street, whose varied topography includes both high ridges and lowlands. And, of course, tunneling through the solid Manhattan schist would not be accomplished by steam shovels or pneumatic drills—both devices still in the future—but shovels and pickaxes driven by the muscle power of thousands of laborers.

The Rapid Transit Railroad commissioners' chief engineer was thirty-five-year-old William Barclay Parsons, a man who, according to *722 Miles* author Clifton Hood, "thought of the subway as a mission rather than a mere job." Two months after the mayor dug out the first shovelful of dirt for the City Hall station, William Parsons posed for photographers on the corner of Bleecker and Greene streets as the engineer drove a pickax between two cobblestones, a signal that the work on the subway was about to begin. Thousands of immigrants, working ten-hour days for twenty cents an hour, began the back-breaking work of digging up the city.

The first order of business was to lay new sewers. Just below the sidewalks was a maze of dirt-encrusted water pipes (some shoved inside of old sewers) mingling precariously with newly laid electric cables and telephone line. Forty-five miles of new sewers would weave up and down beneath the city streets before the men were done.

Below the sewers lay the remnants of the once pristine island, the springs and ponds and streams that the Dutch settlers saw. Laborers became amateur archaeologists. As Benson Bobrick described in *Labyrinths of Iron:* "Huge Mastodon bones were unearthed at the Dyckman Street Station; and near the Battery . . . there emerged the charred hull of the Dutch merchant ship *The Tiger*, which had caught fire and sank in 1613." Along Elm Street workers came upon Aaron Burr's hollowed-out pine logs used as water pipes for the city's first rudimentary aqueduct.

ABOVE: William Barclay Parsons plunging a ceremonial pickax into the earth at Bleecker and Green streets, signaling the beginning of subway construction. Museum of the City of New York.

OPPOSITE TOP: August Belmont, who financed subway cars and equipment for the new Interborough Rapid Transit Company, maintained a strong proprietary interest in the line. © Oscar White/CORBIS.

OPPOSITE BOTTOM: Subway construction in Longacre Square, 1901. By 1904, the Pabst Hotel would be replaced by the NEW YORK TIMES tower and the area renamed Times Square. From the collection of the New-York Historical Society.

Beneath the General Post Office at Park Row, running north to Twenty-eighth Street, lay a series of pneumatic tubes used for the delivery of mail. Great care had to be taken to work around these tubes, since the slightest deviation in alignment would have stopped the mail.

As crews dug huge trenches up Broadway, Fourth Avenue, and Forty-second Street, traffic problems worsened. Along the heavily trafficked avenues and intersections wooden bridges were installed for horsecars and trolleys. Less-traveled streets close to the digging were closed off entirely, causing an economic nightmare for shopkeepers. The gaping holes became moats, keeping customers away. Building foundations had to be shored up. So did supports for the elevateds. At Columbus Circle great care was taken to make sure that the seven-hundred-ton monument to Christopher Columbus did not topple.

If workers caught a break tunneling through the soft soil of Manhattan's southern tip, their good fortune changed once they got to Fourteenth Street, where a ledge of hard rock running close to the pavement extended north for five long blocks. After sinking vertical shafts at either end, sandhogs would dynamite the rock at both ends, foot by seemingly impenetrable foot, until they met in the middle. A bit farther north, at Murray Hill, they came face to face with the eponymous rock formation,

part of a ridge extending from Twenty-seventh to Forty-second Street, rising thirty-plus feet at a sharp forty-five-degree angle. It was also unstable, with large pockets of shattered rock that were an invitation to cave-ins. Further impeding the routing was an old trolley tunnel running beneath Park Avenue. Two separate subway tunnels had to be built through the unpredictable earth to circumvent the existing tunnel running from Thirty-Second to Fortieth streets.

Although William Parsons had decided on the open trench approach to subway tunneling—in which a trench was dug and covered as the tunneling in that segment was finished, the method was used on only half of the subway's length. Manhattan's uneven topography called for some "out-of-the-box" problem solving. At 125th Street, an area known as Manhattan Valley because of the large dip in its surface, a 2,174-foot

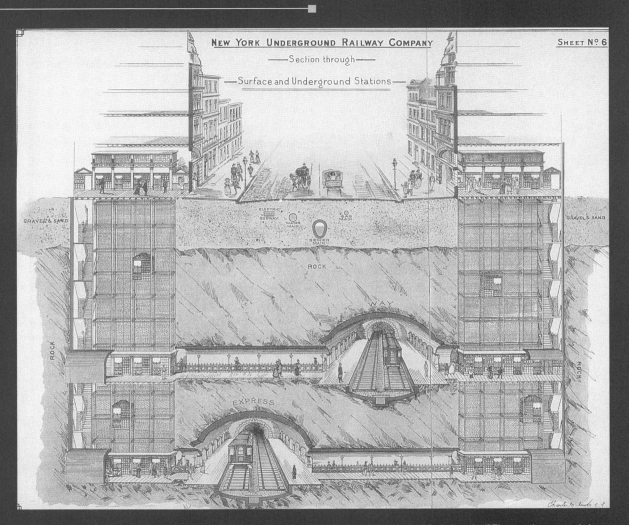

ABOVE: An artist's rendering of the new multilayered city. Horsecars and omnibuses plod along Broadway while, below, the IRT's new subway cars whisk through the new subterranean tunnels. **Museum of the City of New York.** OPPOSITE: The foundation for the NEW YORK TIMES building was being excavated at the same time as the IRT subway tunnels, enabling subway cars to run beneath the building. **Museum of the City of New York, the Byron Collection.**

viaduct was constructed between 122nd and 135th streets. Subway trains emerge from the tunnel at 120th Street and ride the dramatic arch to 135th Street before descending once more belowground. The subway's deepest tunnel was dug at 158th Street in Washington Heights, running for two miles to Hillside Avenue in Fort George. It is so deep that elevators were installed to deliver passengers to the surface at the 168th, 181st, and 191st Street stations.

The tunneling was not only difficult; it was, at times, deadly. On October 24, 1903, near the Fort George portal at 195th Street and St. Nicholas Avenue, sixty feet below the sidewalk in the deepest section of the subway, disaster struck. It was close to ten p.m. when a gang of twenty-two sandhogs, who had spent the day blasting through the solid schist, planted their dynamite sticks and followed foreman Timothy Sullivan to the surface. With only a few hundred feet to go, everyone was anxious to get the job done. It had been standard procedure to set off two dynamite blasts for rock tunneling, but on this stretch of tunnel, perhaps because work was so close to completion, the contractor ordered three blasts. He had apparently not taken into account the fragility of the rock, made porous by underground springs, and the fact that the angle of the Fort George schist, like Murray Hill's ridge, could hide pockets of decayed, shattered rock.

After hearing the three explosions, the workers followed Sullivan back into the tunnel area. Suddenly there were three more blasts, probably from unexploded dynamite. The weakened tunnel roof gave way, loosening a three-hundred-ton boulder that came bounding down on the workers below. Ten men lost their lives, including the foreman, an electrician, and eight Italian workers who were so new to the country that they were identified by numbers instead of names.

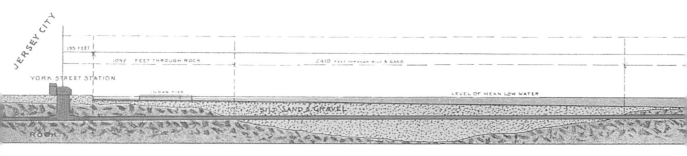

For New Yorkers, construction tragedies marked the darkest element in the tumultuous battlefield landscape they had been enduring for the past three years. They had lived so long with the boarded-over trenches running up and down Fourth Avenue and Broadway, it was difficult to remember when these thoroughfares were passable streets. Now, with just one year to go before they would have their new subway, the citizens of the city felt themselves on the precipice of a new era, one that would see them connected not just to the other boroughs, but to far-off parts of the country.

A companion to the glorious Brooklyn Bridge, the Williamsburg Bridge, was under construction, and two more East River bridges, the Manhattan and Queensboro, were being planned. On the other side of the island, the Hudson River was about to be spanned, not by bridges but by tunnels. In the summer of 1902, construction began on the Hudson & Manhattan Railroad Company's tunnels, through which trains would carry commuters from Hoboken, New Jersey, to lower Manhattan. Years later, we would know these tunnels as the PATH (Port Authority Trans-Hudson) line. Farther uptown, the Pennsylvania Railroad was burrowing through New Jersey's Bergen Hill and under the riverbed. Eventually, its two tunnels would emerge in the city's new gateway, Charles McKim's Pennsylvania Station.

And at Twenty-third Street, where Fifth Avenue and Broadway form a triangle, Daniel Burnham had just given the city its first skyscraper, an oddly shaped building that would forever be dubbed the Flatiron Building. The slender structure resembled a ship's prow, stately and arrogant, as if it was put there to launch the new vertical city. Skyscrapers above and subways below. New Yorkers held their breath awaiting the imminent arrival of their city of tomorrow.

OPPOSITE: August 15, 1901—with subway construction underway at Elm (now Lafayette) Street, sidewalk superintendents peer into the chasm left by the IRT's cut-and-cover method of constuction. From the collection of the New-York Historical Society.

BELOW: By 1902, the Hudson & Manhattan Railroad Company had begun excavation for their tunnels connecting New Jersey with lower Manhattan. From the Museum of the City of New York.

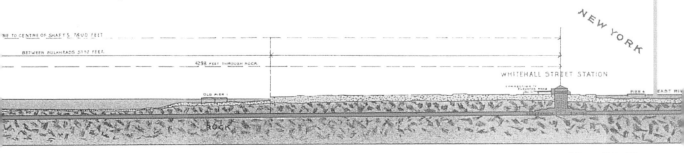

THAT ELEGANT, SWELL-

Much as the subway has been talked about,
New York was not prepared for this scene and it
did not seem able to grow used to it.

NEW YORK TIMES
Friday, October 28, 1904

If ever there was a day for celebration, October 27, 1904, was it. It was a picture-perfect autumn afternoon, bright and crisp. Flags were hoisted, and bunting wrapped the facades of many buildings along lower Broadway. By one o'clock, a crowd of over ten thousand had gathered outside City Hall and stretched all the way back to the Brooklyn Bridge. Inside City Hall's Aldermanic Chamber, speeches were long and solemn. One man, shouting to be heard above the din from the crowd outside, caught the mood of the day: "We are here today for the purpose of turning over a new page in the history of New York!" he bellowed.

One hour and twenty-six minutes later, the newly elected mayor, George B. McClellan, son of the Civil War general, emerged from beneath the flags and bunting to stand at the edge of the steps of City Hall. Waving a silver motorman's key given to him by August Belmont, he announced to the near-hysterical crowd: "I now, as Mayor, in the name of the people, declare the subway open."

EGANT SUBWAY RIDE

Around him played the city's impromptu inaugural orchestra—the tugboat foghorns and ocean-liner bleats, the church bells and factory whistles—as the mayor led August Belmont, John Mac-Donald, William Parsons, and a host of guests the short distance to the City Hall subway kiosk. The new subway's kiosk entrance—the same one that would be used for all IRT entrances—was a fanciful structure of cast-iron and glass with an elegantly rounded roof borrowed from the *kushks*, or "summerhouses," of ancient Turkey and Persia. Down the steps they went below the city's surface, entering what was without a doubt the crown jewel of subway stations. A "cool little vaulted city of cream and green earthenware, like a German beer stein" was how one journalist described it. Spanish architect Rafael Guastavino executed Heins & LaFarge's concept of dramatic sweeping lines, as he spanned the narrow crescent-shaped platform with a series of arches, each wrapped in the Guastavino company's trademark honey-colored terra-cotta tiles laid out in a herringbone pattern. Stained-glass skylights set into several panels in the roof opened the platform to daylight, while brass chandeliers illuminated the station at night.

UNDERGROUND LOOP STATION AT
CITY HALL, NEW YORK

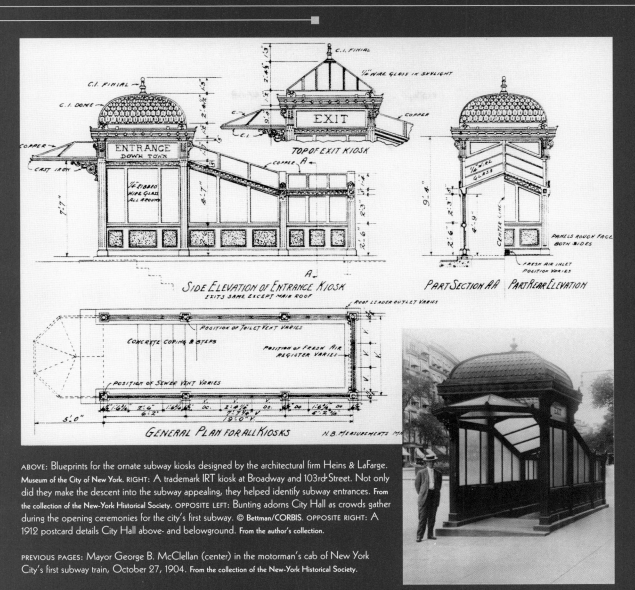

C.I. FINIAL

⅛ WIRE GLASS IN SKYLIGHT

C.I. FINIAL

C.I. FINIAL —

C.I. DOME

EXIT

TOP OF EXIT KIOSK

COPPER

CAST IRON

ENTRANCE
DOWN TOWN

COPPER —

⅛ WIRE
GLASS

COPPER

A

SIDE ELEVATION OF ENTRANCE KIOSK

EXITS SAME EXCEPT MAIN ROOF

¼ RIBBED
WIRE GLASS
ALL AROUND

9'-4"

⅛ WIRE
GLASS

PANELS ROUGH FACE
BOTH SIDES

FRESH AIR INLET
POSITION VARIES

PART SECTION A A   PART REAR ELEVATION

ROOF LEADER OUTLET VARIES

POSITION OF TOILET VENT VARIES

CONCRETE COPING & STEPS

POSITION OF FRESH AIR
REGISTER VARIES

POSITION OF SEWER VENT VARIES

5'-0"

GENERAL PLAN FOR ALL KIOSKS

N.B. MEASUREMENTS MA

ABOVE: Blueprints for the ornate subway kiosks designed by the architectural firm Heins & LaFarge.
Museum of the City of New York. RIGHT: A trademark IRT kiosk at Broadway and 103rd Street. Not only
did they make the descent into the subway appealing, they helped identify subway entrances. From
the collection of the New-York Historical Society. OPPOSITE LEFT: Bunting adorns City Hall as crowds gather
during the opening ceremonies for the city's first subway. © Bettman/CORBIS. OPPOSITE RIGHT: A
1912 postcard details City Hall above- and belowground. From the author's collection.

PREVIOUS PAGES: Mayor George B. McClellan (center) in the motorman's cab of New York
City's first subway train, October 27, 1904. From the collection of the New-York Historical Society.

OPPOSITE: August Belmont, William Barclay Parsons, John B. MacDonald, and Mayor George B. McClellan inspect the new subway tracks on New Year's Day, 1904. *Museum of the City of New York.*

BELOW: At first, the public was outraged to see advertisements nailed into the tiles of their brand-new subway stations. Here ads line the beautiful City Hall station. *Courtesy of A. Sumner-Sackett.*

Waiting at the platform was the city's first subway train. There were five cars with seats for fifty-two passengers. Three of the cars were steel and the remaining two were "composite cars," which were made of wood, sheathed in copper, and painted a deep Tuscan red. With the motorman's controller handle still in his hand and an excited entourage in tow, the mayor was about to realize the dream of millions of New Yorkers. At precisely 30 seconds past 2:35 p.m., after seating himself in the motorman's chair, he inserted the key controller and gave it a turn, setting the train in motion. Through the new tunnel they went, with the IRT's general manager, Frank Hedley, hovering anxiously over McClellan. The mayor, who was supposed to start the train as a ceremonial gesture and then hand over the controls to the motorman, had decided to take the group of dignitaries for a grand ride. Crossing to the

express track just north of the Brooklyn Bridge station, the mayor whizzed past local stations as he raced through the tunnel. "Aren't you tired of it? Don't you want the motorman to take it?" Hedley asked nervously as the train rocketed toward Spring Street. Hedley was worried, not only for the safety of the mayor's guests—the college presidents, archbishops, and bankers—but also for the image a wrecked train would convey to New Yorkers who still harbored some apprehensions at the notion of riding below the sidewalks. "No, sir!" McClellan replied self-assuredly. "I'm running this train!"

Onward they forged, past the Bleecker Street station where happily fortified fans who had gathered at the nearby ten-week-old Subway Tavern cheered them on. "Slower here, slower! Easy!" Hedley

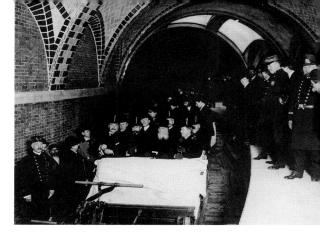

shouted as the mayor, behaving like a teenage drag racer, navigated the train around curves at a dangerous forty miles an hour. At one point in the impromptu journey, the oversized Tiffany controller handle struck the brake handle, bringing the train to a screeching stop and sending the mayor's high-powered guests flying about the cars. Undaunted, the mayor pressed on, up Fourth Avenue to Grand Central Station, where Mrs. William K. Vanderbilt, Jr., sat with her own party of elegantly dressed society matrons at the platform's edge, waiting to wave them on. Rich and poor, young and old, all of New York had gathered to bear witness to the magnificent new subway.

The mayor continued across Forty-second Street to Times Square, and north again up Broadway, where, at 103rd Street, his adolescent dream was played out and he allowed the motorman to bring the train to 145th Street, its last stop. Had McClellan continued to the end, he would have been in for a special treat. The only stretch where New Yorkers could catch a glimpse of the first subway train aboveground is where it runs across the Manhattan Valley viaduct. Here crowds had gathered on rooftops and fire escapes and on every street corner. The twenty-two-mile ride was clocked at twenty-six minutes—eleven minutes more than the heralded "fifteen minutes to Harlem," but given the erratic first run, it was hardly comparable. McClellan spent the return trip to City Hall among his friends, the aura of the urban pioneer about him as he described what it was like to play motorman in the city's new subway.

For the rest of the day, the mayor's guests—fifteen thousand of them—rode the subway free of charge. Then at seven o'clock, after the line was shut down for a brief inspection, the IRT subway was officially opened to the public. Crowds stormed the entrances, parting with their five-cent fares as they pressed down onto the platforms to await the train. Some had come from Brooklyn, others from New Jersey, to take that first ride. From seven until sometime after midnight, over 120,000 people rode the subway on that Thursday evening, descending onto the platforms at the rate of 25,000 an hour. As described by Clifton Hood in *722 Miles*, "the night took on a carnival atmosphere, like New Year's Eve. Many couples celebrated in style by putting on their best clothes, going out to dinner, and then taking their first ride together."

Crowd of guests entering the Subway at the City Hall (Photo by Phillips)

First train leaving City Hall Station (Photo by Paliss)

Mayor McClellan running the first train

First Official Train Run with Mayor as Motorman; 125,000 Take Night Rides

Following Ceremonies of Dedication in the Aldermanic Chamber City Officials and the Men Who Built the Road Ride Over Its Length

England Asks Punishment; Russia Refuses to Yield; France Seeks to Mediate

Lord Lansdowne Insists on Penalties Being Meted Out to Officers Responsible for Firing on British Trawlers

At times crowds were overwhelming. At one point, passengers who rode from City Hall to 145th Street crossed to the downtown platform for the return trip. There they encountered two thousand Washington Heights residents jamming the platform and stairs for their first segment of the subway ride. Through the long celebratory night, a few limbs got crushed and several people complained of dizziness as their eyes peered out the windows and fixed on the rapidly passing tunnel walls. People lost their way, not knowing east from west or north from south when they were underground. Others, unaccustomed to reading the station signs, rode past their intended stops. But all in all, New Yorkers had a wonderful time, knowing that on this night they had taken a ride into history.

In another part of town, in the ballroom of the elegant Sherry's Restaurant at Fifth Avenue and Forty-fifth Street, seventy railroad titans and financiers gathered to celebrate one of their own: the man who underwrote the city's first subway. August Belmont was feted in grand style. At one end of the room, on a large oval table, was a replica of the IRT's Seventy-seventh Street station, embellished with extraordinary details. The ten-foot-wide, forty-foot-long display was, according to Benson Bobrick in *Labyrinths of Iron*, "complete with platforms, stairways, ticket booths, tracks, artificial illumination, tiles, ornamentation, and even colored signal lights." All evening, two four-foot IRT model cars, each with its own toy motorman, entertained guests by running back and forth on electrified tracks.

Throughout the weekend people continued to pour into the new subway. On Sunday, the only day off for most working New Yorkers, close to a million tried to board a system that could accommodate only 350,000 passengers a day. Lines snaked around blocks. "Doing the subway" soon became a catchphrase as people rode it for recreation. A few months before the new year, the Subway Express Two-Step, a dance mimicking the motion of a subway car, swept the city. And in their song "Down in the Subway" composers Jean Schwartz and William Jerome gave young New Yorkers a new place for romance:

Down in the Subway,
Oh, what a place!
Under the isle of Manhattan, speeding through space
Just the place for spooning,
All the season 'round,
Way down, way down in the Subway
Underneath the ground.

August Belmont, who treated the new subway as if it were his personal fiefdom, would often ride in the cars, making sure his motormen powered the trains smoothly and that everything was functioning properly. He was ever on the lookout for ways to solve or minimize concerns that might blossom into runaway problems. Early on, complaints of dizziness, fainting spells, and nausea began surfacing as passengers worried about the

OPPOSITE: The NEW YORK HERALD headlined opening ceremonies, including the mayor's now-famous joyride to 103rd Street and Broadway. General Research Division, the New York Public Library, Astor, Lenox, and Tilden Foundations.

BELOW: Songwriters were quick to put words and music to the new subway experience. Courtesy of the Larry Zimmerman Collection.

OPPOSITE: The October 29, 1904, edition of the NEW YORK HERALD captures the subway experience of first-time riders. General Research Division, the New York Public Library, Astor, Lenox, and Tilden Foundations.

BELOW: Booklets like this one, published in 1909, instructed novice passengers on the intricacies of the subway system. Courtesy of Nancy Groce, NEW YORK: SONGS OF THE CITY (Watson-Guptil, 1999).

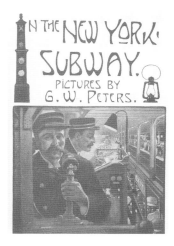

quality of subway air. An article in *The New York Medical Journal*, targeting the unventilated air as a viral chamber for tuberculosis and pneumonia, didn't sit well with already nervous New Yorkers. Belmont lost no time in hiring a Columbia University professor to perform a scientific study of the subway's air quality. By November, a month after the subway had opened, pamphlets were handed out to passengers as they entered the station. Across the cover in bold letters were the words "SUBWAY AIR AS PURE AS YOUR OWN HOME."

New Yorkers loved to ride their subway, but so did out-of-towners who considered it a unique tourist attraction. The subway even blurred class lines, as gowned and tuxedoed couples bound for the theater found it faster than Hansom cabs. And then there was August Belmont, so delighted with his subway line, he ordered a private subway car. Early in 1904 Belmont commissioned the Wason Manufacturing Company of Massachusetts—the same company that built his IRT subway cars— to build the Mineola at a cost of over eleven thousand dollars. Its luxurious interior reflected the exorbitant price tag: Walls were of natural mahogany with brass trim, the arched Empire ceiling was bathed in a tinted pistachio green. Velvet drapes and cut-glass wall vases filled with fresh flowers framed stained-glass windows. The Mineola had its own lavatory, a linen closet, a steward's galley, a kitchen, and a bar where champagne was kept chilled. Built-in leather chairs provided the utmost comfort. The car, which had its own motorman, was kept on a siding accessed through a private entrance in the basement of the financier's Belmont Hotel, which was rising on Park Avenue and Forty-second Street, near Grand Central Station. One of Belmont's great pleasures was to take friends for private subway rides touring the tunnels.

During its first year, 106 million people rode the subway, and there was no reason to think that the numbers would decline. Once the novelty of the new subway was gone, it was replaced by a sense of accepted convenience, as people grew used to the ability to get from place to place with a fair degree of speed and predictability. Even during the dog days of its first New York summer, when temperatures belowground were high and the air was steamy and ripe, New York's enthusiasm for its subway showed no

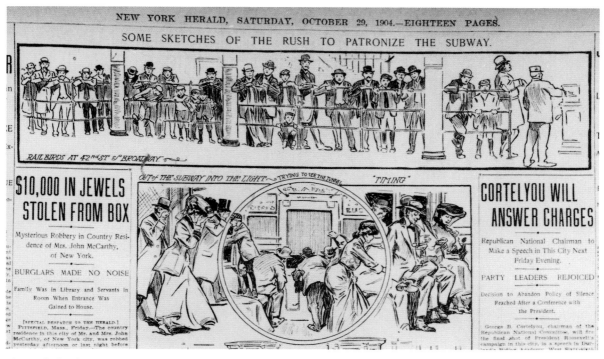

SOME SKETCHES OF THE RUSH TO PATRONIZE THE SUBWAY.

RAIL BIRDS AT 42ND ST & BROADWAY

OUT OF THE SUBWAY INTO THE LIGHT   TRYING TO SEE THE TUNNEL   "TIMING"

$10,000 IN JEWELS STOLEN FROM BOX

Mysterious Robbery in Country Residence of Mrs. John McCarthy, of New York.

BURGLARS MADE NO NOISE

Family Was in Library and Servants in Room When Entrance Was Gained to House.

[SPECIAL DESPATCH TO THE HERALD.]
PITTSFIELD, Mass., Friday.—The country residence in this city of Mr. and Mrs. John McCarthy, of New York city, was robbed yesterday afternoon or last night before

CORTELYOU WILL ANSWER CHARGES

Republican National Chairman to Make a Speech in This City Next Friday Evening.

PARTY LEADERS REJOICED

Decision to Abandon Policy of Silence Reached After a Conference with the President.

George B. Cortelyou, chairman of the Republican National Committee, will fire the final shot of President Roosevelt's campaign in this city, in a speech in Durland's Riding Academy, West Fifty-ninth

sign of abating. Meanwhile, work on the tunnels continued. In July of 1905 the IRT was extended south down Broadway to South Ferry as part of Contract Two. At the South Ferry, the tracks were built so close to the shoreline—literally a couple of feet away—pumps ran constantly in order to keep the water out. A month after the subway opened, trains along the East Side line had already reached Bronx Park, its northern destination. It would be another three years before the West Side line would reach 242nd Street and Broadway.

The subway had changed the city's face, creating neighborhoods far beyond the limited reaches of the elevateds. By unifying and connecting the city, the subway had truly urbanized it. In his speech on the day he opened the subway, Mayor McClellan dismissed the 1898 consolidation of the boroughs as "little more than a geographical expression." For McClellan and for most New Yorkers, Greater New York was born on the same day as the subway, making them the "sons of the mightiest metropolis the world has ever known."

HEY! WHAT ABOUT BROOK

As a child growing up in Brooklyn, the subway took us to this very distant land which we referred to as "the City." You got off the subway at West Fourth Street or Forty-second Street and it was a whole different world.

Dan Klores
film producer

No question about it, the citizens of Manhattan were riding easy. They could slip down into any number of subway stations that ran up and down the east and west sides of their narrow island and board a local or express train to get to wherever they wanted to go in pretty good time. But for the citizens of Brooklyn, it was a whole different story. Even though they resided in the city's largest and most populous borough, with a population of over one million and growing, they might as well have been living in another part of the country. Here was a borough, once the country's third largest city, that was changing nearly as rapidly as Manhattan. Factories now lined Brooklyn's once bucolic waterfront and reached deep into Brownsville, which was becoming so crowded that residents complained that it resembled Manhattan's tenement-choked Lower East Side. Neighborhoods that were once quiet hamlets were now thriving communities taking on the personalities of the immigrants who settled there. Brownsville, which was

TOP LEFT: Flatbush near what is now Tilden Avenue. ABOVE LEFT: This horseshoer on New Lots Avenue near Hendrix Street had a thriving trade in 1900. ABOVE RIGHT: This 1924 ad announcing the breaking up of the Harkness estate into a development urges prospective commuters to "Get Aboard" and move to Brooklyn. Images on this page courtesy of the Brooklyn Historical Society. OPPOSITE: Shoppers crowd onto Belmont Avenue in Brownsville. By 1910 it was a bustling Jewish village reminiscent of Manhattan's Lower East Side. From the Brooklyn Museum of Art, Brooklyn Public Library—Brooklyn Collection.

PREVIOUS PAGES: A snow-covered Manhattan-bound elevated train crosses the upper level of the Brooklyn Bridge above cable cars and pedestrians in 1898. Museum of the City of New York.

already luring Jewish garment workers from the Lower East Side as early as 1887, became more densely settled with the arrival of the Fulton Street el two years later. Bedford-Stuyvesant, a country village at the turn of the century that attracted wealthy scions like F. W. Woolworth, became more urbanized once the elevated stopped there, filling its new brownstones with the ethnically diverse population that would become its hallmark.

A large network of trolley cars, street railways, and elevated trains fanning out into the borough gave its citizens some mobility. This hodgepodge of surface transportation was known as the BRT (Brooklyn Rapid Transit Company), and it stretched into the rural areas of Canarsie and Ridgewood, to Flatbush with its elegant Victorian mansions, and to the emerging seaside communities along the edge of the Atlantic Ocean.

But getting to Manhattan in 1905 was another story. Although there was an elevated train running across the Brooklyn Bridge into Manhattan's Park Row terminal, many Brooklynites had to connect to that line. They also relied on the bridge's cable cars to shuttle them back and forth. To reach those cable cars, commuters would first have to make their way to the great terminal on Sands Street at the foot of the bridge. The cable-car ride took only five minutes, but once commuters left the bridge, they would make their way to the City Hall station where the choice was to ascend another flight of stairs to catch the Second or Third Avenue el or descend into the new IRT subway. Either choice required another fare.

ABOVE: Although song-writer William E. Slafer composed the "Brooklyn Daily Eagle Bridge Crush March," a contest was held in 1917 for a song promoting advertising space on the BRT. The prize song was "I Saw It in the BRT." Left image courtesy of Nancy Groce from NEW YORK: SONGS OF THE CITY (Watson-Guptil, 1999) and right image courtesy of the Larry Zimmerman Collection.

OPPOSITE: Trolleys were still a fixture along Brooklyn's Flatbush Avenue (circa 1920) long after the subway arrived. Courtesy of the Brooklyn Historical Society.

Fortunately for Brooklyn, the Board of Rapid Transit Railroad Commissioners was on the case. One year after Belmont's IRT launched, the commission decided that the city needed more subway lines: not just three or four lines, but nineteen of them running through every borough except Staten Island. They envisioned four north-south lines running from the Battery to upper Manhattan, plus crosstown subways intersecting the city at four main thoroughfares. They also proposed three East River crossings reaching into Brooklyn and Queens: 165 miles of tracks, an enormous network compared to the modest twenty-two miles that made up the IRT's run.

This did not put a smile on August Belmont's face. What the BRTRC saw as inevitable expansion, the man who ran the IRT saw as competition. Although he took great pride in the operation of his subway, micromanaging everything from his cars' upkeep to the way his motormen ran them, he didn't much care that people were packed into them like so many sardines. Those sardines were adding to his wealth, and new lines, he argued, would mean fewer profits. And even though developers were buying up large tracts of Bronx farmland in anticipation of the extended subway, Belmont figured myopically that since the subway didn't generate much traffic north of Ninety-sixth Street, it probably never would.

Belmont was willing to throw the RTC a few bones. He planned a spur up Lexington Avenue from Grand Central Terminal. And with the Pennsylvania Railroad's new station rising at Thirty-third Street and Seventh Avenue, he proposed laying more tracks on the Lower West Side. As for getting trains into Brooklyn, Belmont would have a tunnel running beneath the East River, providing express service from the IRT's South Ferry station to Brooklyn's Atlantic Avenue by 1908.

For now, Brooklyn-bound commuters could make do with the Brooklyn Bridge cable cars and trolleys, the el that crossed the bridge, or one of the ferry lines that still ran between Brooklyn and the southern tip of Manhattan. In Belmont's mind, he owned the subways (the IRT was actually owned by the city and leased to Belmont), and if new lines were going to be built, he should be the one to build them.

So when on December 22, 1905, the Manhattan Railway Company, which owned all of New York City's elevateds, put in a bid for the new lines, Belmont bought them out, creating a new company, the Interborough-Metropolitan. To Belmont's chagrin, the Public Service Commission, which had replaced the Rapid Transit Commission, came up with an even more ambitious subway plan. They called it the Triborough System, since subway tracks would reach deep into Brooklyn over the new Manhattan and Williamsburg bridges and also into the Bronx. Unfortunately, that plan was put on ice when no company came forward with money to construct, equip, and operate the lines. Belmont was gloating . . . but not for long.

On November 18, 1910, William McAdoo, president of the Hudson & Manhattan Railroad Company, the man who had just started the Hudson (now PATH) trains running beneath the Hudson River, proposed an even more ambitious plan than the Triborough's: McAdoo wanted to link the new subway with his tubes, making it easier for New Jersey commuters to get to their jobs in Manhattan.

New Jersey! An anxious Belmont decided to trump him.

Belmont's Interborough would build two new subways, one running down the West Side from Times Square to the Battery, where it would cross the East River into Brooklyn. The second route would go up Lexington Avenue from Grand Central Terminal into the Bronx. The Interborough's routing would now resemble a giant H with the crossbar of the shape forming the new shuttle tunnel that would run along Forty-second Street between Times Square and Grand Central Terminal. Belmont had actually outsmarted himself. In taking the bait to outmaneuver his competitor, he defeated his own argument and proved the case for an extended subway system.

With all of these plans floating about, no one had heard from Brooklyn. Not until a man named Edwin W. Winters arrived at the table. As president of the BRT, Winters wanted more than anything to consolidate his lines and bring them to the slender island that Belmont claimed for himself. Winters submitted his plans, and they were not modest. Like Belmont's IRT, Winters's BRT would run from the Battery to Fifty-ninth Street by way of Broadway and Seventh Avenue. At Fifty-ninth Street it would veer east and enter Queens over the Queensboro Bridge.

While the merits of each plan were debated by the Public Service Commission (PSC), Manhattan's borough president, George McAneny came up with a brilliant idea: Why not combine the best that each company had to offer? On June 13, 1911, he formally proposed that the city join with the IRT and the BRT in a dual system to construct the eighty-seven miles of subway track route, each assuming a proportionate share of the $123 million cost. Belmont balked, still trying to hold on to his monopoly. Concessions were made, people grumbled, but in the end, McAneny's proposal was accepted.

On March 19, 1913, in the Tribune Building, just a short stroll from his prized City Hall station, Belmont's Interborough entered into contract with Brooklyn Rapid Transit, both agreeing to lease their planned city-owned subways for forty-nine years and to share the construction and operation costs of the expanded system. With this, the term *dual contracts* (or *dual system*) became part of the lexicon of the New York subway. "City Slicker and Country Bumpkin" could have described Belmont's image of this shotgun wedding. For New Yorkers, the marriage promised to be a magnificent union.

The citizens of Brooklyn were especially pleased. They were finally being put on the city map. In addition to entering Manhattan over the Manhattan and Williamsburg bridges, their BRT would now take them through an East River tunnel from Montague Street in Brooklyn

Heights to Whitehall Street in lower Manhattan. It would continue up Broadway to Fifty-ninth Street, eventually entering another East River tunnel at Sixtieth Street to deliver them to Astoria and Corona in Queens.

Brooklyn's DeKalb Avenue would become a vital nexus where passengers could take any number of subway lines into the heart of the borough. Fourth Avenue, a major artery near the borough's eastern shore, would get a subway line running past the docks and warehouses of Bush Terminal into the high-end community of Bay Ridge. That line would tentacle off to three other lines: the West End, Sea Beach, and Culver lines, all former steam railroads rebuilt and ready to deliver passengers to Coney Island. A second major subway line would connect with the Brighton Beach line, delivering city folk to more sea breezes and beaches.

As for Belmont's IRT, it would cross the East River at Forty-second Street through the Steinway Tunnels, exiting in Long Island City. Named for the piano manufacturer who had backed them, these tunnels, which had been built in 1907 for trolley cars shuttling between Manhattan and Queens, were never put into use. At Queens Plaza the plan was to consummate the BRT-IRT marriage by having both systems share elevated tracks into Astoria and Corona. The IRT's Lexington Avenue and Seventh Avenue lines would also invade Brooklyn, meeting at Borough Plaza where they would branch off to the Nostrand Avenue line, whose last stop was Flatbush Avenue, and the Livonia Avenue line to New Lots Avenue.

Once again, as workers descended into layers of old New York, the dig became at times an archeological one. At Chambers Street and Broadway a crew made a macabre discovery. Here, in the sandy subsurface, human skeletons were found—relics from a Revolutionary War cemetery. Beneath one of Trinity Church's yard retaining walls, contractors came upon an old Dutch well walled in with stone, a leftover from early days in New Amsterdam. Nearby was a human skull, possibly one that managed to roll out of the Trinity cemetery.

As something new was completed, something old had to go. As workers tunneled between Park Place and Murray Street, they broke into Alfred Beach's old pneumatic

ABOVE: A pennant celebrating the ground-breaking ceremonies on October 26, 1912, for the extension of the Brooklyn subway to Bay Ridge. Courtesy of the Brooklyn Historical Society.

OPPOSITE: A postcard depicting the Brooklyn "dual system" subway running 94-feet below the East River. From the author's collection.

ABOVE: Beach's old tunnel revealed by BMT construction in 1912. Museum of the City of New York.

OPPOSITE: One of the BMT's Standards or "Sixty-seven footers." Straphangers appreciated the spacious, wide-bodied cars. Courtesy of A. Sumner-Sackett.

tunnel. It was no surprise. The contractors knew it was there. It was now just something that stood in the way of progress.

One would think a sense of camaraderie would have developed as the IRT and BRT shared the greater task of delivering to New York City the best subway system in the world. That was not going to happen. These two partners were not only foregoing a tranquil relationship with each other, they were determined to lead separate lives. The two systems rarely intersected, and the few connections from one system to the other involved long passageways and transfers that were not free. Because the tunnels did not all have the same dimensions (the BRT required wider tunnels to accommodate their wide-bodied trains) the IRT and BRT could not use the same size of subway car.

In a battle of one-upmanship, the BRT came out with their new "sixty-seven-footers," supplementing their old bulky wooden cars with sleek, all-steel cars. These wide-bodied brown-and-black cars soon became known as the Standards, and are considered to this day to be "the single best piece of rapid transit rolling stock ever produced." Not only were they wider than the IRT cars, the Standards were sixteen feet longer, translating into more seats for passengers. The competitiveness between the two lines amuses New York City subway historian Joe Cunningham: "New York has always been a dual city and the dual contracts reflect that. Manhattan has its own federal courts. Brooklyn has its federal courts. At one time, baseball and newspapers and, to a certain extent, colleges and radio stations were separate. This is a dual city."

The two lines did take time out for celebrations when they each completed their work, coincidentally within a week of each other. On June 19, 1915, a warm, sunny Saturday, at 1:30 in the afternoon, a group of public officials boarded one of the BRT's new sixty-seven-footers under the Municipal Building at Chambers Street. From there they rode to Canal Street, then over the Manhattan Bridge and through Brooklyn's new Fourth Avenue subway tunnel to Sixty-fifth Street on the edge of Bay Ridge. There they switched to the Sea Beach tracks and, in exactly forty-five minutes, arrived at Coney Island. Three days later, on Tuesday, June 22, at 10:45 in the morning, another group of officials boarded an IRT train at Grand Central Terminal and rode through a Steinway tunnel to Jackson Avenue in Queens. That ride took a much shorter three and a half minutes. Both lines formally opened precisely at noon on June 22.

And so, it was accomplished. This fractious marriage between the Interborough and Brooklyn Rapid Transit gave New Yorkers a subway system that would be the envy of London and Paris. At last, Brooklynites living just across the river in Brooklyn Heights or in the still rural reaches of Canarsie could hop a train and come to "the city" for a day's work or a night's pleasure. In his memoir, *A Walker in the City*, Alfred Kazin wrote of how the subway connected him to Manhattan:

> *It was from the El on its way to Coney Island that I caught my first full breath of the city in the open air. Groaning its way past a thousand old Brooklyn red fronts and tranquil awnings, that old train could never go slowly enough for me as I stood on the open platform between the cars, holding on to the gate.*

As for Manhattanites, they could now board a subway at Chambers Street and forty-five minutes later be indulging in one of Brooklyn's tastiest pleasures: a couple of "red hots," better known as Nathan's hot dogs, downed on Coney Island's soon-to-be-famous boardwalk. All of this for the price of a nickel. How sweet was that?

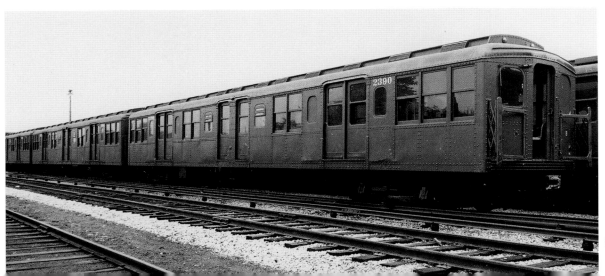

FROM ORCHARD STREET

The newcomers found a neighborhood of streets
overcrowded with people and pushcarts. They lived
crammed into slum tenements.

THE LOWER EAST SIDE REMEMBERED & REVISITED
Joyce Mendelsohn

It was called Trains Meadow, although it had nothing to do with trains. It was an Eden of sorts, where, in 1909, "barns and bee hives, carriage-houses and corn cribs" drew Manhattanites escaping the noisy city. Six wealthy families who wintered in Manhattan owned the half dozen large farms in the area. One family, the Barclays (of Manhattan's Barclay Street) built a racetrack for their trotters on what is now Northern Boulevard between Seventy-second and Seventy-fourth streets. Day-trippers out for a day at the races or a short commune with nature would catch a ferry at Thirty-fourth Street and from there board a streetcar in Long Island City, which ran along Jackson Avenue (now Northern Boulevard) as far as Flushing. They would alight at Trains Meadow amidst the rolling fields and streams, where they could hunt or fish or simply bird-watch.

This was the land that developer Edward Archibald MacDougall had his sights on for another kind of Eden: Here on 325 acres of farmland, between the settlements

TO GREEN PASTURES

59

of Newtown (now Woodside) and Corona, he would build America's first garden-and-cooperative-apartment community and call it Jackson Heights. What made MacDougall decide to act on his ambitious project in this area of meadows and salt marshes was the fact that an IRT line would one day run from Manhattan straight out to Flushing. "Originally, Jackson Heights was planned to face Northern Boulevard, near the Jackson Avenue trolley line," says architectural historian Barry Lewis. "When they announced that the elevated subway was to be built along the new Roosevelt Avenue, the whole plan was turned around."

MacDougall wasn't the only entrepreneur who saw gold in the impending Manhattan connection. Cord Meyer, another developer who was also amassing land for his new Forest Hills in central Queens, was buying up the southern part of the Trains Meadow—part of Newtown—where the entire British army marched after the Battle of Long Island in 1776. He would rename it Elmhurst. And in 1910, Woodside's Thompson Avenue, an old two-lane country road, was expanded into a major thoroughfare in anticipation of an influx of residents and given the name Queens Boulevard. Articles in local Queens newspapers reported how farm after farm was being bought up by the hot new real-estate market, all in anticipation of the new subway line.

In 1900, two years after it became one of the five boroughs of Greater New York, only 4 percent of New Yorkers lived in Queens. At the turn of the century the city's largest borough was actually a vacation spot, so underdeveloped that it had become a popular weekend getaway. But all that was about to change. In 1909, the year that

MacDougall formed the Queensborough Corporation, which would build Queens's new upscale suburb, the Queensboro Bridge was completed, spanning from Fifty-ninth Street in Manhattan to Long Island City in Queens. Eight years later, the IRT would arrive at the new Bridge Plaza (now Queensboro Plaza), a gigantic four-platform, eight-track, two-level major junction not far from the Queensboro Bridge. Here, along with the Second Avenue el trains, the IRT and BRT trains would meet and share tracks to Astoria and eventually to Flushing. This confusing system continued until 1949, when the BRT (now the BMT) got the Astoria route and the IRT became the Flushing line.

And there was Pennsylvania Station, rising in Manhattan a few blocks from the Hudson River, another project that would change the landscape of Queens. In 1901, before construction on the new station had begun, Alexander Cassatt, Pennsylvania Railroad's president, bought controlling shares in the Long Island Railroad, then a suburban line whose tracks ended on the Queens side of the East River. Cassatt would now burrow under the East River, bringing LIRR trains into his new Pennsylvania Station. And because the station was really a terminus for Pennsylvania Railroad trains, the railroad needed a maintenance yard where trains could be cleaned and restocked for the return journey. A 206-acre site in Long Island City was purchased and named Sunnyside Yards after the neighboring community. Eventually, the Long Island Railroad, the IRT, and the IND (Independent) subways would converge at Woodside, transforming farmland into "the transit hub of the borough."

The extension of the IRT and BRT into Queens was meant to alleviate the crowded living conditions in Manhattan, but no one expected to accommodate the 1.3 million immigrants who had streamed into Ellis Island in 1907—the largest migration in world history—most of whom had settled into Manhattan's grossly overcrowded Lower East Side; one thousand people per acre. "Why worry about them? They

PREVIOUS PAGES: Flushing, in the heart of Queens, in 1922. From the Queens Borough Public Library, Long Island Division, Eugene Armbruster Collection.

OPPOSITE: Now criss-crossed with the fourteen-lane Queens Boulevard and six subway lines, Queens was still quite rural in 1923. Shown here are Forrest Hills (TOP), Jackson Heights at Eighty-first Street (CENTER), and Trains Meadow Road (BOTTOM). From the Queens Borough Public Library, Long Island Division, Eugene Armbruster Collection.

BELOW: Pennsylvania Station, completed in 1910, brought Long Island Railroad trains into Manhattan. From the author's collection.

didn't have any money," mocked Queens historian Vincent F. Seyfried, citing the prevailing attitude. For these people, subway or no subway, Jackson Heights was light-years away.

Edward MacDougall's Garden City community was to be a haven for the upper middle class, with eight tennis courts, a six-hole golf course, and a clubhouse where affluent professionals could mix and mingle. "They (MacDougall's Queensboro Corporation) created the first country club community focused on young professionals. Sort of the Yuppies of the Twenties," says Daniel Karatzas, author of *Jackson Heights: A Garden in the City.* Apartments were large and airy in beautifully landscaped buildings. Mother enjoyed bridge clubs, while Father hopped one of the new subway cars for his twenty-two-minute ride to his office in Manhattan. Barry Lewis tapped into the childhood memories of a ninety-year-old former Garden City resident who, as a young girl, had accompanied her mother to see her father off as he headed for the Eighty-second Street subway station: "All around us were these black-suited, bowler-hatted men pouring into the station to get on the subway to go to Wall Street." MacDougall gave residents spacious suburban living in an urban environment, with all the trimmings. "A Continuous Vacation" was how one ad tried to sell it, one that was possible if Mother and Father had lots of dough and weren't Jewish, of course. Jackson Heights was a restricted community, assuring exclusive apartment owners that only their kind would be allowed to buy there.

As for the "wretched, tempest-tossed" immigrants, the Jews and Italians crammed into the Lower East Side and parts of Greenwich Village. By the 1920s, they, too, were taking the subway home, not

to Orchard Street but to Brooklyn, the Bronx, and yes, Queens. Because of the subway, new ethnic neighborhoods were formed, not by developers but by Jews, Italians, and Poles who followed their own to burgeoning immigrant areas. Jews gravitated to Brooklyn's Boro Park and Brownsville. Italians went to Bay Ridge, Canarsie, and South Ozone Park. "If you take these places out of New York City and put them in the middle of Kansas, they would be a major city," says Barry

JACKSON HEIGHTS

Plaza Hotel

Times Square

Herald Square

City Hall

16 Min. to Jackson Heights

22 Min. to Jackson Heights

24 Minutes to Jackson Heights

36 Minutes to Jackson Heights

CENTRAL PARK

25ᵗʰ STREET JACKSON HEIGHTS STATION

New Fireproof Elevator Co-Operative Apartments under construction at Jackson Heights
A. J. Thomas, Architect
J. G. White Engineering Corporation, Builders

New Quick Subway Service
by
B.R.T.–Broadway Line
to
Jackson Heights

New Garden Apartments Now Served by Three Lines of Rapid Transit—B.R.T.—I.R.T. & 2d Ave. "L"

Running Time

5th Avenue at Central Park to Jackson Heights	16 minutes
Theatre District—42nd Street	22 minutes
Shopping District—34th Street	24 minutes
Downtown Office District—City Hall to Jackson Heights	36 minutes

Jackson Heights Elevator Garden Apartments, 5, 6, and 7 rooms, 2 and 3 bathrooms, are offered on the Jackson Heights Tenant-Ownership Plan. Liberal terms arranged for those whose social and business references are acceptable. Residents at Jackson Heights are now enjoying the golf course, tennis courts, children's playgrounds, gardens, etc.

The Queensboro Corporation Manhattan Office 50 East 42d St.
Murray Hill 7057

SELECT YOUR APARTMENT NOW
For Immediate or Fall Occupancy

Broadway B. R. T. Subway from any Manhattan Station direct to Jackson Heights. Take Corona train at Queensboro Bridge Plaza.
Interboro Subway to Grand Central Station transfer to Queensboro Subway (Corona Line) to 25th St., Jackson Heights.
By Motor 59th St. via Queensboro Bridge, Jackson Ave. (Northern Boulevard) to 25th St., Jackson Heights.

LEFT: An advertisement for the new exclusive garden apartments rising in Jackson Heights shows how quickly the subway can deliver commuters to major areas in Manhattan.
Courtesy of Vincent Seyfried.

OPPOSITE: VIPs inspect Borough Hall's new tracks on January 9, 1908, as part of the opening-day ceremonies for Brooklyn's new subway. From the Brooklyn Museum of Art, Brooklyn Public Library— Brooklyn Collection.

ABOVE: Broadway and Eightieth Street in the 1880s (TOP). From the collection of the New-York Historical Society. Today, that same intersection is a bustling thoroughfare (BOTTOM). From the author's collection.

OPPOSITE: The subways became the great assimilators. Artist Isaac Friedlander captures the scene in this 1939 etching. Museum of the City of New York.

Lewis. "These were small American cities because of the subways."

In Manhattan, no neighborhood changed more dramatically as a result of the IRT subway than the Upper West Side. When the elevated arrived in 1879, casting its cinders and shadows across Columbus Avenue, single-family row houses and tenements popped up with stores to serve the still-grand mansions along West End Avenue and "the Boulevard." The IRT's arrival transformed Broadway, West End Avenue, and Central Park West into an enclave of large luxury apartment buildings luring the wealthy and upper middle class from their private homes. At the IRT's Eighty-sixth Street stop rose the thirteen-story Belnord, considered when it opened in 1909 to be the world's largest apartment building, beating out the Apthorp at Seventy-ninth Street, which had a sweeping courtyard and dual carriage entrances.

Another neighborhood was rising in upper Manhattan, one that was born out of overzealous speculation. Riding on the building boom that had transformed the Upper West Side, developers who had purchased lots near the IRT's stop at 135th Street and Lenox Avenue suddenly found themselves with nice apartments but no buyers. Middle-class Manhattanites might be lured to Eighty-sixth Street, but 134th Street, even with the new subway, was not going to happen. For black New Yorkers anxious to leave the West Sixties where they coexisted uneasily with Irish immigrants, opportunity was knocking, and black realtor Philip A. Payton, Jr., was there to help open the door. Payton convinced desperate white landlords to rent their apartments to black tenants, which they were happy to do at greatly inflated rents. By 1914, fifty thousand black New Yorkers were living in Harlem, laying the groundwork for the vibrant Harlem Renaissance in the 1920s.

Meanwhile, in the Bronx all the farmland that speculators had purchased prior to Belmont's IRT was now covered with six-story apartment buildings. Because developers wanted to make a quick turnaround on their investments, they decided to build for working-class New Yorkers, creating what were deceptively called new-law tenements. Not to be confused with the small, airless tenements from which these workers were escaping, these new buildings, rising along the IRT's Broadway and Lenox Avenue branches, contained spacious apartments with two bedrooms, private bathrooms, and lots of light. It may not have been Jackson Heights with its golf course and tennis courts, but for the factory worker coming from his overcrowded Manhattan tenement, it represented "a way station on the road to the middle class." By 1913, Italians, Yugoslavians, Armenians, and large groups of central and eastern European Jews had made the move north into the Bronx.

The subways became the great assimilators, as blue-collar and white-collar workers rode shoulder to shoulder. For everyone, the magic ticket was the five-cent fare. "That nickel subway was true to the end of the line," says Barry Lewis. "This meant that the people who were pulling themselves up from the lower middle classes could take that nickel subway and if they went far enough, they could find cheap enough land for a place to live." It also meant that middle-class suburbanites ran for the hills as the foreign hordes began arriving in their neighborhoods. First-class or steerage, everyone was affected by the subway.

And they all went to Coney Island. For one nickel, both the middle class and the poorest of the poor who endured the stifling city heat in crowded, airless tenements could escape on the subway. In 1864 developers had visions of genteel resorts sitting grandly along Brooklyn's oceanfront where elegant

vacationers in straw hats and white suits would arrive to enjoy sea breezes. They even named Brighton after a tony seaside resort in England. The Brooklyn Flatbush and Coney Island Railroad (later the Brooklyn and Brighton Beach Railroad), a steam railroad built in 1878, was ready to deliver the resort's clientele to the upscale Brighton Beach Hotel. Nearby Coney Island's three theme parks—Steeplechase Park, Luna Park, and Dreamland—all

charged admission and catered to the middle class. But by 1920 when the new subway service was linked to the refurbished Brighton Surface line, Coney Island became accessible to all New Yorkers. The surf was free, as were a handful of bathhouses, and by 1923 when Coney Island's famous boardwalk was built, a million people would flock to its beaches on a hot summer Sunday.

Not surprisingly, the once crowded borough of Manhattan had become a bit of an empty nester, having sent its brood off to the other boroughs where they were thriving and multiplying. By 1930, Brooklyn, the borough that once longed to get its BRT trains into Manhattan so that it could be part of the action, now had more people than any of the five boroughs. Brooklynites were also no longer riding the BRT. By 1918, just a few short years after signing the dual contracts, Brooklyn Rapid Transit had gone into receivership. World War I and its whiplash inflation was a factor. Another was the Malbone Street wreck, one of the worst disasters in subway history. On November 1, 1918, with a strike enveloping the BRT, an overtired, inexperienced crew dispatcher with minimal motor training was ordered to run the Brighton Beach train to Park Row in Manhattan and back again to Brighton Beach. On the return trip, the crowded train raced down an incline to a sharp S curve, derailing as it approached a concrete tunnel. As many as one hundred and two people were said to have perished as the wooden cars collapsed into piles of splinters.

Although the wreck was disastrous enough to force the city to rename Malbone Street as Empire Boulevard, the disaster wasn't the straw that broke the BRT's back. The big one was the five-cent fare. When the IRT and BRT signed on the dotted line, they also signed on for a fixed fare that would remain that way for an astounding forty-nine years, regardless of inflation. A subsidy from the city would have helped, keeping the ride affordable to the poor while the company stayed solvent. But both the IRT and BRT were private companies, and red flags were raised at the mention of any government interference.

There was also another problem: The city's mayor, John F. "Red Mike" Hylan, who had taken office in 1917, hated the BRT. The story goes that when Hylan was a law student he took a job as a BRT motorman, and was fired for taking a curve too fast. The grudge-bearing Hylan thwarted the line's attempts at expansion, gave the thumbs-down to a much-needed repair shop and storage yard, and refused to budge on raising the crippling fare. Finally, in 1923, the Brooklyn Rapid Transit was reorganized as the Brooklyn Manhattan Transit Corporation, the BMT.

Meanwhile, the IRT, in spite of red ink caused by inflation and that frozen five-cent fare, was extending its Flushing line. By 1926, a station along the line opened in Manhattan at Fifth Avenue and Forty-second Street, and a year later you could also catch a Queens-bound IRT at Times Square. Finally, on January 21, 1928, the line was completed with the opening of the Flushing Main Street station.

By the time the IRT reached Flushing in 1928, the sun had set on the well-heeled gentry of Jackson Heights. The distant rumblings of the Great Depression would soon become a resounding crash, and the days of chasing balls on a private golf course were numbered. Apartments would be subdivided, with some of them rented out as furnished rooms. Furnished rooms in snooty Jackson Heights! The golf course would vanish, so would the eight tennis courts, and by the time the Depression was over, Jackson Heights would be transformed into the middle-class urban neighborhood it resembles today. Before that came to pass, however, New Yorkers would get a third subway system, one that not only covered the avenues, streets, and boulevards the IRT and BMT had left behind, but a system that would be instrumental in bringing sunshine back onto their streets.

OPPOSITE LEFT: A day at the beach in 1954 for New Yorkers, who had only to hop a subway for the delights of Coney Island. OPPOSITE RIGHT: Coney Island's boardwalk in 1910 before its famous wooden one was built and before the subway brought all classes to the amusement park. ©Bettman/CORBIS.

THE AVENUES OF EX

You must take the "A" train
To go to Sugar Hill way up in Harlem.
If you miss the "A" train
You'll find you missed the quickest way to Harlem.

"Take the 'A' Train"
Billy Strayhorn

All of Harlem understood its importance. Years before Duke Ellington and Billy Strayhorn's evocative "Take the 'A' Train" gave America a lyrical geography of the black community just south of Washington Heights, Harlem experienced a renaissance, and people of all creeds and colors soon knew of Harlem's famous writers, artists, and jazz clubs. Ellington and his orchestra were making good noise at the Cotton Club, and at the block-long Savoy Ballroom where all of Harlem was "stompin'," the sweet sounds of the Fletcher Henderson's Orchestra were riding over the radio airwaves into living rooms all over America.

The people of Harlem knew that a subway line reaching up from the Hudson terminal at Chambers Street to 207th Street, straight through the neighborhood's spine, was much more than a convenience. It was, according to Ric Burns and James Sanders in *New York: An Illustrated History*, "an avenue of expansion, connecting, in the process, the tenements of upper Manhattan

to the spacious brownstones and apartment houses of central Brooklyn." By the late 1920s the last of the Jews and Germans had abandoned Harlem, settling into the new apartment houses along West End Avenue and Riverside Drive. Although there were black New Yorkers who had attained enough wealth to move to the upscale town houses that defined Sugar Hill and Strivers' Row, most Harlem residents were pressed into dreary, overcrowded tenements. Now the new IND line would deliver Harlemites of every status to new neighborhoods in Brooklyn, particularly to Stuyvesant Heights (now Bedford-Stuyvesant), one of the few communities where they could afford to buy their own homes. Originally settled by freed slaves, Stuyvesant Heights' population exploded once the IND reached the area in 1936, making it the largest black community in New York City to this day.

Oddly, the subway line that Mayor Hylan touted as his "people's subway," hyping it for newsreel cameras and WNYC Radio's microphones during ceremonies to herald the beginning of the system's construction in March 1925, got very little attention when it opened seven years later. Hylan had even chosen John Hancock Park at the intersection of St. Nicholas Avenue and West 123rd Street, a patch of greenery in the black community, for the ground breaking. This was, after all, his pet project: an independent subway, city-owned and city-run, free from the tentacles of his two enemies, the privately run IRT and BRT. Even its name, the Independent, telegraphed what had become his obsession.

But at midnight on September 10, 1932, with just sixty seconds to go before the first Eighth Avenue subway line was to begin operation, there wasn't a mayor in sight. Ex-governor Al Smith had managed to arrange a celebratory breakfast at the New Yorker Hotel, on Thirty-fourth Street and Eighth Avenue, directly above an IND subway stop. The West Side Association of Commerce was there. So was the Harlem Board of Commerce. But no mayor. There were no marching bands or ribbon cuttings at turnstiles, just the gathering of straphangers with nickels in hand, anxious to be among the first to try out their new subway.

Much had happened in New York City during the seven years since that silver pickax plunged into the earth in John Hancock Park. By 1932 "Red Mike" Hylan was history, and the mayor who succeeded him, the charming, crowd-pleasing Jimmy Walker, had taken up the cause of the IND subway and made it part of his election campaign. "Say it with shovels," Walker declared. Once elected, Walker kept his promise to build the Independent's Eighth Avenue subway, but when the city got the bill for it—a whopping $800 million—rumors spread that their lovable rascal of a mayor had pocketed some of the proceeds to support his extravagant nightclubbing lifestyle. "The city did not get what it paid for. Although it certainly paid for what it got," proclaimed financial adviser Joseph D. Goldrick. Walker's reputation for financial mischief had finally caught up with him, forcing his resignation in 1932, and just twelve hours after the Independent subway opened its turnstiles to the public, the Italian liner *Conte Grande*, which had anchored at Fifty-seventh Street and the Hudson River, just a few blocks west of the IND's Fifty-ninth Street subway stop, would carry him into exile.

By 1932, the year the IND began the first leg of its service, New Yorkers had grown accustomed to a city that was more cosmopolitan and accessible. Earlier, in 1927, the same year Coney Island got its Cyclone, Clifford Holland dug a tunnel ninety-four feet below the Hudson between Manhattan and New Jersey, not for trains, but for Mr. Ford's automobiles. On January 21, 1928, Mayor Jimmy Walker led a parade up Fifth Avenue to celebrate the opening of the IRT's final stop at Main Street on its Flushing line. Six months later, five thousand residents in Brooklyn's

PREVIOUS PAGES: Crowds gathering outside Harlem's landmark Savoy Ballroom in 1952. It was the IND's Eighth Avenue line that helped open up black Harlem to the rest of the city. © Bettman/CORBIS.

OPPOSITE: Billy Strayhorn's 1941 classic puts the importance of the IND's A train from Harlem to music. Courtesy of Nancy Groce, NEW YORK: SONGS OF THE CITY (Watson-Guptil, 1999).

LEFT: The arrival of the IND subway line in Queens was a cause for celebration. Dignitaries pose at a ribbon-cutting ceremony at Broadway and Roosevelt Avenue in 1932. From the Queens Borough Public Library, Long Island Division, Borough President of Queens Collection.

B'way S. at Roosevelt Ave.

ABOVE: The subway made the Brooklyn Paramount on Flatbush and DeKalb avenues accessible to teenagers who went there to see the Platters and Bill Haley and His Comets in the 1950s. Courtesy of the Brooklyn Historical Society.

OPPOSITE: Workers shoring up the tunnel for the IND's Sixth Avenue line. Museum of the City of New York.

Ridgewood section held their own parade celebrating the arrival of the BMT line in their neighborhood. That year, the opulent Brooklyn Paramount opened on Flatbush and DeKalb avenues, close to all subway lines. Its first feature was, appropriately, *Manhattan Cocktail.* Eight years later, residents of Harlem would see their wish come true when the Eighth Avenue subway linked Harlem to Bedford-Stuyvesant.

The Independent subway was conceived as a city line, and although it would serve the Bronx, Brooklyn, and Queens, its primary purpose was not to reach into new, uncharted neighborhoods. Hylan, who wanted more than anything to give the IRT and BMT a run for their money, decided that the best way to beat the two lines was to join them. Competition was clearly on Hylan's mind when the IND's subway map was drawn up.

The Eighth Avenue subway would parallel the IRT's Broadway line, traveling with it neck and neck from Manhattan's southern tip to Fifty-ninth Street and Columbus Circle. From there it would take a more easterly route, hugging the edge of Central Park West, beneath the elegant apartment houses, until it reached 155th Street, the northern edge of Harlem. At that point the IND would form a giant Y with one line flaring west, close to the Hudson River at 168th Street and Washington Heights. The other line would cross the Harlem River, where it would once again travel neck and neck with the IRT, this time along the Bronx's Grand Concourse, past Tremont Avenue to 205th Street, a short distance from the IRT's last stop at Woodlawn Cemetery. It is in Woodlawn Cemetery where a marker stands above the remains of sixty-four Revolutionary War soldiers, transferred there by the Board of Transportation after they were unearthed during excavation for the IND's train yards and repair shops.

As for the BMT, Hylan's primary enemy, it would soon feel the heated breath of competition. Crossing the East River via a tunnel south of the Brooklyn Bridge, the

IND would enter bustling downtown Brooklyn before traveling along Fulton Street through black Bedford-Stuyvesant, Jewish Brownsville, and finally the melting pot of East New York. Not content with Brooklyn, the IND would invade Queens through a tunnel under the southern tip of Welfare Island, just south of the BMT's Sixtieth Street tunnel. From there it would enter Queens Plaza, a maze of converging tracks, before looping around the factories of Steinway Street in Long Island City as it traveled on past Woodside under Queens Boulevard to suburban 179th Street and Hollis, Queens.

Nothing prepared the sandhogs for what they were up against on March 15, 1936, when excavation for the IND's Sixth Avenue line began. No question about it, everyone was anxious to see a new subway line running up Sixth. Although just one block west of elegant Fifth Avenue, it was little more than "a grubby collection of four- and five-story brick tenements whose storefronts were occupied by cheap restaurants, furriers, barbershops, and drug companies." It was the Sixth Avenue el casting its constant shadow that had frozen this major thoroughfare in the commerce of yesterday. Not surprisingly, realtors were anxious to upgrade the avenue, knowing that a subway line would make the grimy, noisy elevated obsolete.

Mayor Fiorello LaGuardia, just a year into his term, rolled up his sleeves and asked the federal government for a $60 million loan, the estimated cost of building a Sixth Avenue subway line. Half of that money was needed to move the Hudson & Manhattan Railroad terminal from Thirty-third Street to Thirty-second Street. This was necessary so that the IND's tracks could run alongside the H&M tracks from Eighth to Thirty-third Street. Aboveground, streetcar service was halted as the tunnels were being dug. And because the el needed to be kept running, its 670 support columns had to be reinforced. After relocating the labyrinth of subterranean utility lines,

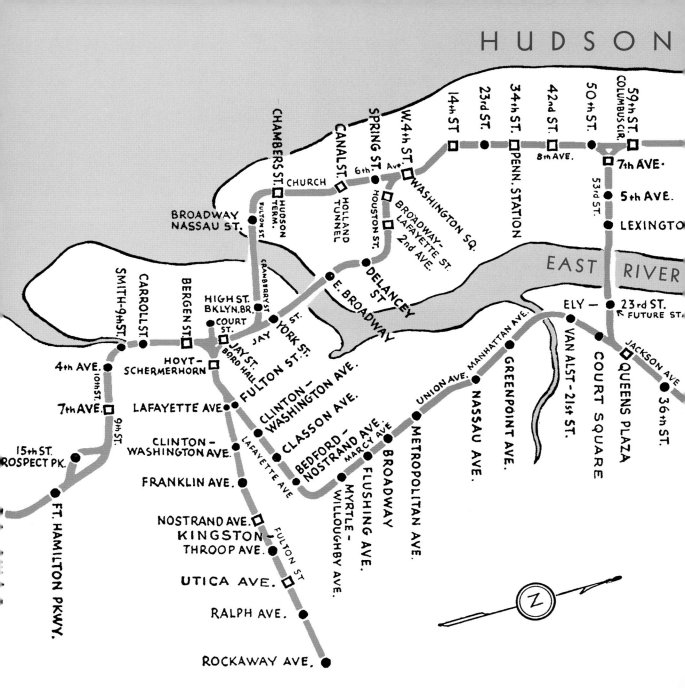

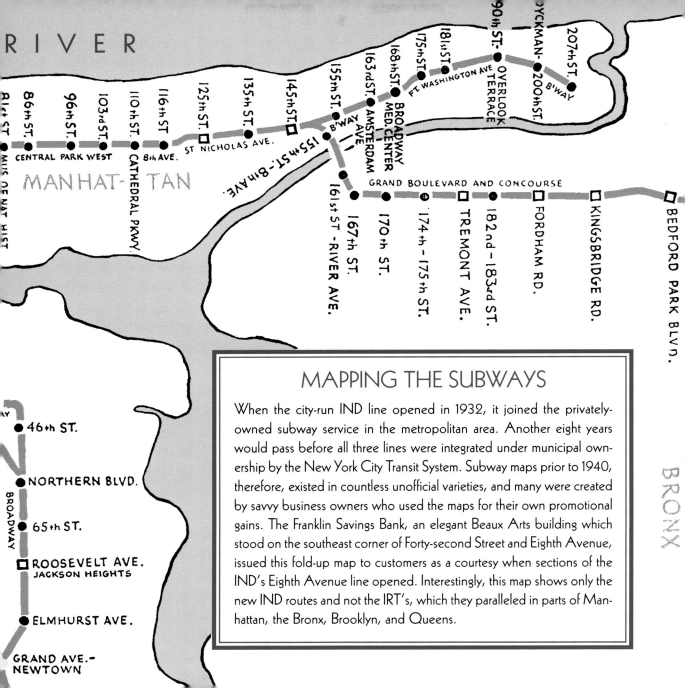

RIVER

MANHAT-TAN

BRONX

86th ST. · 96th ST. · 103rd ST. · 110th ST. · 116th ST. · 125th ST. · 135th ST. · 145th ST. · 155th ST. · 163rd ST. · 168th ST. · 175th ST. · 181st ST. · 190th ST. · DYCKMAN-200th ST. · 207th ST.

81st ST. MUS OF NAT HIST

CENTRAL PARK WEST · CATHEDRAL PKWY. · 8th AVE. · ST NICHOLAS AVE. · B'WAY · AMSTERDAM AVE. · BROADWAY MED. CENTER · FT WASHINGTON AVE · OVERLOOK TERRACE · B'WAY

155th ST-8th AVE.

155th ST-8th AVE.

161st ST - RIVER AVE. · 167th ST. · 170th ST. · 174th -175th ST. · TREMONT AVE. · 182nd-183rd ST. · FORDHAM RD. · KINGSBRIDGE RD. · BEDFORD PARK BLVD.

GRAND BOULEVARD AND CONCOURSE

46th ST.

NORTHERN BLVD.

BROADWAY

65th ST.

ROOSEVELT AVE.
JACKSON HEIGHTS

ELMHURST AVE.

GRAND AVE.-
NEWTOWN

MAPPING THE SUBWAYS

When the city-run IND line opened in 1932, it joined the privately-owned subway service in the metropolitan area. Another eight years would pass before all three lines were integrated under municipal ownership by the New York City Transit System. Subway maps prior to 1940, therefore, existed in countless unofficial varieties, and many were created by savvy business owners who used the maps for their own promotional gains. The Franklin Savings Bank, an elegant Beaux Arts building which stood on the southeast corner of Forty-second Street and Eighth Avenue, issued this fold-up map to customers as a courtesy when sections of the IND's Eighth Avenue line opened. Interestingly, this map shows only the new IND routes and not the IRT's, which they paralleled in parts of Manhattan, the Bronx, Brooklyn, and Queens.

cables, and mains, huge ledges of Manhattan schist were carefully blasted, removed, and carted off to Riker's Island. With the city already densely built up, IND tunnels had to connect the unused West Fourth Street's lower level multilevel tracks, pass over an aqueduct and the Pennsylvania and Long Island Railroad tracks at Thirty-third Street, and run between the H&M tracks and under the BMT tracks at Thirty-fourth Street. The task was, according to Groff Conklin in *All About Subways*, "one of the greatest engineering feats man has ever accomplished."

Four years later, on December 14, 1940, Mayor LaGuardia presided over the official opening of the Sixth Avenue line. If the opening of the Eighth Avenue line eight years earlier was sadly unsung, this subway inaugural mimicked the ceremony that the mayor's predecessor George McClellan hosted thirty-six years before at City Hall. In fact, John D. Rockefeller, Jr., one of the mayor's two thousand invited guests attending the celebration, had ridden the first IRT line on its opening day in 1904. "I rode in the first city subway many years ago," he boasted, "and I have been using the subways ever since."

At twelve minutes before midnight, the mayor appeared at the Thirty-fourth Street station with his two thousand guests in tow, snipped the red-white-and-blue ribbon that had been stretched across the turnstiles, and announced: "I now formally open the Sixth Avenue subway and dedicate it to the public use." Dropping a nickel into the turnstile, LaGuardia led his guests down an escalator to the uptown-train platform where two special trains awaited them. Both trains proceeded nonstop, arriv-

ing at Rockefeller Center at one minute before midnight, where celebrations were planned into the wee hours of Sunday morning.

The mayor and his guests were ushered through mezzanines and corridors into Radio City Music Hall and then on to the nearby Center Theatre, where a program of entertainment was planned to celebrate the subway opening. At one point, radio announcer Ben Grauer, who was serving as master of ceremonies, paid tribute to Mayor LaGuardia: "For last Christmas he gave us 'No El, No El,' and for this Christmas he gives us the splendid new subway." Grauer was referring to another ceremony the mayor had performed two years before. On another December day in 1938,

LEFT: The Sixth Avenue el was abandoned on December 4, 1938. Two years later, the IND Sixth Avenue subway replaced it. From the collection of Andrew Grahl.

the mayor stood on the corner of Sixth Avenue and Fifty-third Street, acetylene torch in hand as he posed for photographers. The torch was one of many that would be used to dismantle the Sixth Avenue el.

"Long, broad and brilliantly lighted" was one reporter's description of the IND's mezzanine that ran between Thirty-fourth and Fortieth streets. Although this particular corridor was designed purposely to serve the nearby Fifth Avenue department stores, all the IND stations had wide platforms and generous, well-lighted mezzanines. The Independent had learned the lessons of the IRT, whose platforms, especially the one at Seventy-second Street and Broadway, were very narrow. After all, the city's own subway was planned with the idea that all those straphangers who had been riding the quickly vanishing elevateds would now be descending into its stations.

Then, on June 1, 1940, one of Hylan's never-realized dreams was about to come true, when a BMT subway car bearing Mayor LaGuardia and his wife, Marie, entered the Times Square station and emitted three short blasts of its horn, signaling the moment when the BMT subway became the property of the New York City Transit System. By June 12, the city would own the IRT as well. Now, with the city owning every mile of subway, including Brooklyn's elevated lines, what

OPPOSITE: Mayor Fiorello LaGuardia poses in a BMT motorman's cab on June 1, 1940, celebrating the unification of the city's three separate subway systems under municipal control. Fiorello H. LaGuardia Collection: La Guardia & Wagner Archives. Copyright held by International New Photos Inc. (UPI).

RIGHT: A 1940 cartoon that appeared in an IRT advertisement announcing public ownership of the transit system. Courtesy of A. Sumner-Sackett.

OPPOSITE TOP AND CENTER: Crowds watch as Brooklyn's Fulton Street el comes down on June 16, 1941, making way for the new IND subway. From the Brooklyn Public Library—Brooklyn Collection.
OPPOSITE BOTTOM: The Ninth Avenue el would continue to run until 1940. From the collection of Steven Zabel, courtesy of Eric Oszustowicz.

had occurred was nothing less than the largest railroad merger in U.S. history.

With unification came the freedom and the power to make great strides in the development of the subway and, in turn, the city itself. First to go were the outmoded els, except for a small section that ran from Rockaway Avenue to Leffert's Boulevard until April 26, 1956. Brooklyn's Fulton Street el made its final run on May 31, 1940, each station dimming its lights in homage as it rattled by. Twelve days later, both the Ninth Avenue el and the Second Avenue el above Fifty-ninth Street were shut down. In Manhattan "silence" parties were held as the ugly noisemakers were dismantled. The only el left standing was the one running on Third Avenue, but everyone knew its days were numbered.

In 1929, as the IND was being built, plans for the Second Avenue subway were drawn up. The line was to run from Houston Street to the Harlem River, not far from where the Third Avenue el still rattled along. At Thirty-fourth Street a crosstown subway would burrow under a new East River tunnel, delivering commuters to Queens. But as developers tinkered with the routes, the stock market crashed, shelving the plans for a Second Avenue line.

Decades later, in 1968, those plans would be taken down and dusted off, with new routes from 34th to 126th Street put on the drawing board. Three years later, routes would extend south again to Whitehall Street. On October 27, 1972—appropriately the sixty-eighth anniversary of the opening of the city's first subway—Governor Nelson Rockefeller and Mayor John Lindsay, along with Senator Jacob Javits and U.S. Secretary of Transportation John Volpe, gathered at East 103rd Street and Second Avenue for the ceremonial ground breaking. Optimism was in the air as New Yorkers imagined the convenience of finally riding that long-awaited line. Streets and sidewalks between the Bowery and Chrystie Street, from East 99th to East 105th Street, and from East 110th to East 120th were dug out as excavation began. Four years after the work had begun, a fiscal crisis paralyzed the city, extinguishing any hope of completing the new Second Avenue line. The tunnels were covered over and sealed.

Fortunately, plans for the Second Avenue subway have not been permanently buried. The day is on the horizon when New Yorkers traveling up and down the east side of Manhattan will have another subway line, lightening the burden of August Belmont's original IRT and changing the face of the ever-expanding city.

NEW YORK'S LOVE-HATE RELATIO

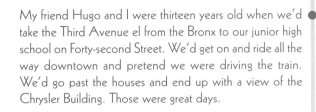

My friend Hugo and I were thirteen years old when we'd take the Third Avenue el from the Bronx to our junior high school on Forty-second Street. We'd get on and ride all the way downtown and pretend we were driving the train. We'd go past the houses and end up with a view of the Chrysler Building. Those were great days.

Dominic Chianese
actor

Everyone who remembers the Third Avenue el has a story—sometimes framed in the rosy glow of nostalgia, often tinged with images of the shadows it cast. Long after the subway took its place, Third Avenue's noisy, sun-blocking behemoth, frozen in the city's past, still had a hold on its present. The avenue it concealed was locked into a rough-edged pallor, yet the lacy patterns formed by steel and sunlight along the rutted streets remain a definitive and cherished image of the city of yesteryear. Its presence gave sharp boundaries to neighborhoods that changed with the length of a city block. Life along Third Avenue under the el's shadow was vastly different from Lexington Avenue, just a block west. When Ray Milland, as the alcoholic writer in *The Lost Weekend*, tries to pawn his typewriter, he visits an actual pawnshop on 106th Street, one of many lining the avenue. Under cover of the el, pawnshops and saloons seemed to own the neighborhood.

"The Third Avenue el was the dividing line between

RIGHT: Boys of summer opening a hydrant on Ninety-fifth Street. This photograph originally appeared in BY THE EL, THIRD AVENUE AND IT'S EL AT MID-CENTURY by Lawrence Stelter with photography by Lothar Stelter (H&M Productions, Flushing, NY: 1995).

the rough neighborhoods and the better ones," says Tom Begner, a physician's son who grew up on Madison Avenue in the 1950s. Begner remembers how threatening the Third Avenue kids seemed whenever he ventured to Rappaport's, a popular toy store on Third Avenue and Seventy-eighth Street. "Third Avenue was different from everything else because of the el," says Begner. "You just didn't go there."

For radio personality Jonathan Schwartz, who had to circumvent its huge pillars to get to the Beverly Theater on Fiftieth and Third Avenue, it was a demarcation zone. "I never took the el. To me it was a foreign animal. I avoided it as I would an unpleasant drunk at a party." But for Anita Rodriguez Dowers, who grew up on Third Avenue during the 1950s, the el becomes the focus of a warm memory: "My father, who worked nights, rode the el to work. Each afternoon at four he would board the train, and when it passed by our window, my mother and I would wave to him."

For passengers, a ride on an el often became a serendipitous tour of the city. High above the sidewalks and removed from traffic, one sat back and took in the sights as the streetscape glided by. Dr. Edward J. Bottone spent many a lazy summer day doing just that. "As kids we didn't have much to do, so we'd sneak on at 116th Street and just ride the trains. It was an adventure."

Imagine riding thirty to forty feet above the narrow, winding streets of lower Manhattan at eye level with the second stories of buildings along the way. After negotiating the curve along the East River docks and the old countinghouses of Coenties Slip, the train would skirt Manhattan's financial towers as it carried you up to Chinatown's Chatham Square where, according to Dr. Bottone, "you could reach out and almost touch the buildings." In his short story "Death in the Air," mystery writer Cornell Woolrich describes the experience of riding the el as it rattled past Greenwich Street: "The old mangy tenements closed in on it on both sides of the cars as they threaded through them. There was, at the most, a distance of

PREVIOUS PAGES: "Sunshine and shadow" best describes the effect the Third Avenue el had on the street below. The photograph originally appeared in BY THE EL, THIRD AVENUE AND ITS EL AT MID-CENTURY, by Lawrence Stelter with photography by Lothar Stelter (H&M roductions: Flushing, N.Y., 1995).

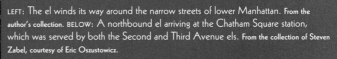

LEFT: The el winds its way around the narrow streets of lower Manhattan. From the author's collection. BELOW: A northbound el arriving at the Chatham Square station, which was served by both the Second and Third Avenue els. From the collection of Steven Zabel, courtesy of Eric Oszustowicz.

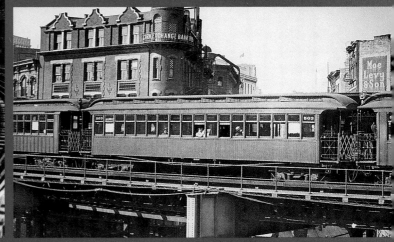

HANOVER SQUARE NEW YORK

ABOVE: The Third Avenue el at the Canal Street stop. Note the wooden cars and the wooden platform. RIGHT: The Ninth Avenue el at 110th Street and Central Park West, turning into the famous "Suicide Curve." The famous structure was abandoned in 1940. Both photographs from the collection of Steven Zabel, courtesy of Eric Oszustowicz.

three yards between the outer rail of the superstructure and their fourth-floor window-ledges, and where fire-escapes protruded only half that much." From Chinatown it would travel past Grand and Houston streets along the Lower East Side, then up to tenement-lined Third Avenue. At Ninetieth Street it would ride past the Ruppert Brewery, a series of orange brick buildings stretching to Ninety-third Street where the smell of malt would waft into the cars. The old Ninth Avenue el went to 110th Street and Morningside Park where the train would rise a dramatic sixty-three feet above the sidewalk—the tallest point in the city—as it screeched along the great serpentine, or "suicide," curve.

For New Yorkers, the seasons were keenly experienced on an el train. Rocky Doino was a twelve-year-old eighth grader living on 112th Street and Third Avenue when he was dispatched to run a weekly errand: "On Sundays after mass I had to go down to Grand Street to pick up ravioli for my mother. I remember in the winter the seats, which were covered in a type of hard canvas, were very, very cold. There were lots of local stops, so it took forever to get there." For Josephine Francendese, who rode the el from 106th Street to Chatham Square, the summertime made a trip on it a unique experience: "I would ride outside between the chains to catch the breeze. We had no air-conditioning then, so all the apartment windows along the way would be open. And of course people living in those apartments weren't wearing very much." New Yorkers who lived in the tenements along the avenues where the els passed—especially in apartments with sight lines to the trains—sacrificed privacy to become part of an urban sideshow. They also usually paid less rent.

Still, there was an odd coziness about these giant structures. Beneath the eaves of the iron staircases, newspaper stands and vendors set up shop. Upstairs, in the waiting room, a potbellied coal stove warmed hands and feet during the winter's chill. "When it was cold outside, the person who manned the ticket booth would shovel coal in the stoves," says Jimmy Skellas, who can

LEFT: In Berenice Abbott's 1936 el station photograph, passengers huddle around the pot-bellied stove as they wait for their train. Museum of the City of New York.

OPPOSITE TOP: Passengers wishing to switch from the subway to the el were issued paper transfers. Courtesy of A. Sumner-Sackett.

OPPOSITE BOTTOM: The el station at Fifty-ninth Street was equipped with an enclosed escalator protecting Bloomingdale's shoppers from the elements. This photograph originally appeared in BY THE EL, THIRD AVENUE AND IT'S EL AT MID-CENTURY by Lawrence Stelter with photography by Lothar Stelter (H&M Productions, Flushing, NY: 1995).

still hear the sizzling sound the coals made. A snowfall on the tracks would give the edgy avenue an unexpected serenity. In the sunlight those wooden tracks seemed to unfold like a road to Oz.

Photographers were captivated by the el, from the famous New York City chroniclers Berenice Abbott and Andreas Feininger to the unknown Lothar Stelter, whose melancholy color photographs of the Third Avenue el, captured in the book *By the El: Third Avenue and Its El at Mid-century*, transport the viewer back in time. Ashcan School artists Everett Shinn, John Sloan, and Reginald Marsh illustrated the structure's place in the emerging modern city in their paintings.

Hollywood loved the el. As early as 1928, when most filming was done on its

RIGHT: A production still from THE LOST WEEK-END (1945) with Ray Milland riding an el after pawning his typewriter. FAR RIGHT: Third Avenue el tracks at East Fifty-eighth Street. Notice the pawnshop sign with the signature three globes above. Is this where Ray Milland left his typewriter? Both photographs from Photofest.

OPPOSITE: New Yorkers had mixed feelings about the demise of the el. This last run of the Third Avenue el marked the end of these trains in Manhattan. This photograph originally appeared in BY THE EL, THIRD AVENUE AND IT'S EL AT MID-CENTURY by Lawrence Stelter with photography by Lothar Stelter (H&M Productions, Flushing, NY: 1995).

back lots, Harold Lloyd shot a scene for his movie *Speedy* under the el, incorporating into the script an actual collision of a trolley with one of the el's iron columns. And who can forget 1933's *King Kong*, when the giant ape's enormous eyes peer into a passenger car after ripping up the tracks of the Sixth Avenue el? The el's grating whine echoed the desperation of the alcoholic character Ray Milland played in *The Lost Weekend* (1945) as he made his way to another Third Avenue saloon. The jury's verdict in Sidney Lumet's *12 Angry Men* literally hung on what was seen in a tenement window. So was the plot in Woolrich's "Death in the Air," in which a detective riding the Sixth Avenue el witnesses a passenger's murder caused by a bullet fired through a window. In the story, whose plot was loosely borrowed by Alfred Hitchcock for his film *Rear Window*, the guilty party doesn't stand a chance: "'I saw you,' said Step, 'through the window from an "El" train.'"

When the els first arrived in the 1870s, they were functional as well as fashionable. In lower Manhattan there were single tracks along the edge of the sidewalks allowing the sun to bathe the center of the street. The depot houses were fanciful Victorian structures described by Robert Reed in *The New York Elevated* as "incredibly rich and inviting in their pretty, ornamental gingerbread, romantic peaked gables, lacy iron balustrades, fancy eaves, quaint cupolas topped with finials, and Corinthian capitals on iron pillars." Painted an apple green with maroon trim, they resembled fanciful cottages. The waiting rooms had blue-and-crimson stained-glass windows, adding a genteel charm while taming the sunlight.

New York Times reporter Meyer Berger tapped the memory of Samuel J. Bloomingdale, son of the department-store founder, in his book *Meyer Berger's New York*. Bloomingdale, who was born in 1873, remembered the el in its early days: "The Third Avenue line carried gentry as well as poor folk downtown to Wall Street and South Ferry. No one laughed at the elevated railroad then. It was new and rather grand." Bloomingdale was saddened at the way "folk came to scoff at its potbellied stoves and stained-glass windows," remembering that they were part of a "rich era, and wonderful for their time."

Because of its impact on the city, it wasn't surprising that when the last Third Avenue el train made its final run on Thursday, May 12, 1955, from Chatham Square to 149th Street, one could see people—the sad and the curious—lining the avenue. From tenement windows people waved as the worn wooden cars crawled by. One woman on Ninety-sixth Street turned a mop into an impromptu flag. As the el made its final run, stopping along the way, people kept trying to hop aboard the six-car train, already packed with photographers, newsmen, and fans of the elevated. A trio with a pitcher

of martinis, who had tried unsuccessfully to board, raised a toast from one of the platforms. It was a day full of high emotion. There was even an eleventh-hour court order, obtained by Michael J. Quill, the irascible Transport Workers Union president, to prevent the el's demolition. That proved fruitless. For better or worse, something that had helped shape the city was about to vanish. "The elevated trains followed street cars and double-decker Fifth Avenue buses into the limbo of outmoded public transportation," a *New York Times* reporter wrote. Rocky Doino remembers going off to war in the 1950s and when he returned the Third Avenue el was gone. "Third Avenue was flooded with sunlight," he remembers. "All those run-down stores were being replaced with newer ones." Something lost, something gained. Isn't that the story of the city?

NEW YORK'S TROLLEY

I went to lose a jolly hour on the trolley
and lost my heart instead.

"The Trolley Song"
Hugh Martin

New York City a trolley town? It's odd picturing twentieth-century Manhattan with trolley cars plying its streets, but up until 1948 when the last trolley made its final run, they were everywhere. If the rumble of the els above was a familiar sound, so was the clang of the trolley. Four years after Frank Sinatra enraptured thirty thousand bobby-soxers in Times Square's Paramount Theater, networks of thin iron tracks embedded between the city's Belgian blocks still threaded their way around Manhattan. Trolleys ran along every major crosstown street, often from river to river, across Central Park, around Columbus Circle, over all four East River bridges, under the els, through the Park Avenue tunnel beneath Grand Central Terminal and up and down most of Manhattan's avenues. There were trolleys on short hops running along Eighth Street from Avenue A to Sixth Avenue, and trolleys with runs that took passengers from the Polo Grounds in upper Manhattan to Center Street in lower

SONG

Manhattan. They were also very convenient and often preferred by Manhattanites to the Third Avenue el, which ran above them. "I took them often," says Josephine Francendese. "With the el you had to climb the stairs. I could just hop on and hop off the trolley."

A character eluding the police in Cornell Woolrich's short story "Dusk to Dawn" decides that a trolley is his best means of escape:

He took a street car down as far as Chatham Square. He had a feeling that he'd be safer on one of them than on the El or the subway; he could jump off in a hurry without waiting for it to stop, if he had to.

Two companies, the Third Avenue Railway with its red-and-cream-colored trolleys, and the New York Railways with its green ones, filled the city streets. Because of a city ordinance instituted after the blizzard of 1888, which banned all overhead wires, Manhattan trolleys drew their power from conduits below the streets. The one exception were the lines that ran along 181st Street between Broadway and Washington Bridge.

There was a sense of whimsy about these vehicles. For a time, colorful "hobble-skirted" trolleys—so named for their flared bottoms—traveled along Broadway. At one time Broadway had the "Broadway Battleship," a double-decker trolley that resembled a kiddie ride, sweeping along the Great White Way. In the summer the windows on trolley cars were replaced by screens reaching down to floor level. Some "open bench" cars had no screens or windows, permitting passengers to jump into a seat right from the street.

PREVIOUS PAGES: The BROOKLYN EAGLE shot this picture of passengers boarding a Flatbush and Atlantic Avenue trolley in 1940 to protest the narrow sidewalk. Overhead is the abandoned Fifth Avenue and Culver BMT. From the Brooklyn Public Library—Brooklyn Collection.

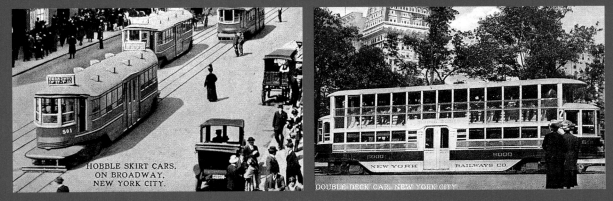

HOBBLE SKIRT CARS,
ON BROADWAY,
NEW YORK CITY.

DOUBLE-DECK CAR, NEW YORK CITY

ABOVE LEFT: The colorful hobble-skirted trolleys, introduced in 1914, making their way up Broadway. ABOVE RIGHT: One of the double-decker trolleys popular in the early part of the twentieth century. Above photographs from the author's collection. RIGHT: Riders peering out of trolley car windows in 1902 watch in fascination as construction is under way for the Lexington Avenue IRT. Courtesy of Al Gilcher.

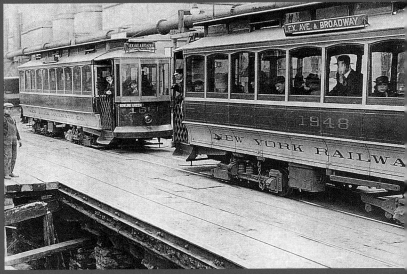

OPPOSITE TOP: A Forty-second Street trolley heading west. The Ninth Avenue el is in the background. From the author's collection. OPPOSITE CENTER: A red-and-cream Third Avenue trolley making a turn at Columbus Circle. OPPOSITE BOTTOM: In the 1940s you could take a trolley to the Paramount Theater to catch a movie. From the collection of Andrew Grahl.

"It was nice in the warm weather because you could get some air," remembers William Bromberg, who rode the Broadway line as a young boy. Some kids, like the young Dr. Bottone, intent on by-passing the five-cent fare, had their own way of riding the trolleys. "We would hitch on the back of them. You just jumped on and hung on for a few blocks. The conductor would always be chasing us."

These descendants of the 1870 horse-cars that once plodded up and down the streets of Manhattan captured the hearts of New Yorkers as soon as the first electrified trolleys arrived on the scene at the turn of the century. The entrepreneurial trolley companies tapped into the new incandescent lighting so that at night their cars became a great attraction. Henry Collins Brown describes them in his book *In the Golden Nineties:* "For a trifling expense a car could be illuminated from one end to the other in a perfect blaze of multi-colored lights, producing at once a carnival spirit that was quite irresistible." In Brooklyn, people organized "trolley parties," starting a fad that spread to other boroughs, while Manhattanites who rode these trolleys just for the fun of it with no destination in mind became the city's first "pleasure-riders."

The people of Manhattan loved their trolleys, but up until the 1950s, the citizens of Brooklyn could hardly imagine life without them. In the 1940s there were forty-nine trolley lines stretching into places no subway could go. One line, the Norton's Point Line, actually passed through the back alleys of Coney

Island's bungalow colony, through its own special gate into the exclusive Sea Gate community where its tracks ran right into the ocean. During World War I, soldiers left Brooklyn from this point, jumping from the trolley and walking along a connecting wharf where steamers waited to carry them across the Atlantic.

Trolleys were so much a part of Brooklyn, the borough named its baseball team after them. Long before Brooklyn became one of the five boroughs, when it was still a separate city, the citizens of Brooklyn were referred to as "trolley dodgers" because they spent half their lives getting out of the way of the trolleys that seemed to claim their streets. The term became a part of Brooklyn lore, and the name of the borough's baseball team was changed from the Superbas to the Brooklyn Trolley Dodgers. The word *trolley* was dropped after a time, and the team became known as the Brooklyn Dodgers.

Long before the subway came to Brooklyn, years before the Brooklyn Bridge spanned the East River, horsecars and cable cars brought Manhattanites from Brooklyn's Fulton Street at the edge of the East River, where the ferry dropped them, to the then upscale oceanside resort of Brighton Beach. By the early 1890s, it was the Brooklyn trolley that delivered masses of melting New Yorkers to Coney Island's shore, people looking for amusement would flock to the racetracks of Coney Island and Brighton Beach. So many trolleys arrived at Brighton Beach that a trolley ter-

ABOVE LEFT: A Bergen Street trolley in the heart of downtown Brooklyn. The building on the left housed the headquarters of the Dodgers. ABOVE RIGHT: Brooklyn residents ride a Green Hornet trolley in 1934. Above photographs courtesy of A. Sumner-Sackett.

OPPOSITE TOP: In 1896 canvas shades were the only form of air-conditioning on the Nostrand Avenue trolley at Atlantic Avenue in Brooklyn. Courtesy of the Brooklyn Historical Society.

OPPOSITE BOTTOM: An 1898 advertisement introducing Brooklynites to the trolley, "with its elegance, comfort and ease," a far cry from the "clatter and rattle" of horsecars. Courtesy of the Brooklyn Historical Society.

OPPOSITE: Luna Park, Coney Island's 1903 fantasy land. From the author's collection.

minal was built there. "A century ago Brooklyn had the biggest and most popular ocean resort in the United States," says Brooklyn Borough Historian Ron Schweiger. None of that could have happened without those trolleys.

Into the mid-1950s, trolleys that were part of the Sea Gate line ran along Coney Island's Surf Avenue, giving day-trippers a tour of the Cyclone and the Wonder Wheel, Steeplechase Park, and the famous B&B Carousel. As a ten-year-old, Ron Schweiger took the Coney Island Avenue trolley to Brighton Beach with his grandmother. "The trolley would go down this alleyway almost to the boardwalk. I remember the sound of the bell when you wanted to get off and the screech of the steel wheels against the rails." That line ended in a trolley barn on West Fifth Street. Inside was a carousel to entertain the children who were waiting for trolleys to take them back to their neighborhood.

If you wanted to catch a double feature at the Brooklyn Paramount or RKO Albee in downtown Brooklyn, you had only to hop a trolley running along DeKalb Avenue. That same trolley would bring you into Brooklyn Heights and over the Brooklyn Bridge into Manhattan. Brooklyn trolleys ran along Ocean Avenue, past the stately homes of Flatbush, to the famous Lundy's seafood restaurant at Sheepshead Bay. They could be found in every kind of neighborhood, interconnecting most sections of Brooklyn with their

ABOVE RIGHT: Men board the trolley for a day at the Brighton Beach Racetrack in 1897. Museum of the City of New York, the Byron Collection. RIGHT: The Sea Gate trolley rides along Coney Island's Surf Avenue in the summer of 1946. Courtesy of A. Sumner-Sackett.

network of silver tracks. In the 1940s, Larry Karlin was a rookie patrolman about to board the Fifth Avenue trolley when a woman who had lingered too long at a saloon managed to get up the trolley's step, where she stalled. "I gave her a nudge," says Karlin, "and since the trolley was on the way to the station house, I brought her in."

By the late 1940s, these charming, slow, noisy trolley cars were coming to the end of their line as buses began replacing them. For Manhattan's New York Railways green line, the end came first. On June 8, 1936, after finishing its Eighty-sixth Street crosstown run, the company's last trolley pulled into the trolley barn on Eighty-fifth Street and Madison Avenue, and the doors were closed. Twelve years later, the Third Avenue Railway's red-and-cream cars had vanished from Manhattan streets. Brooklyn held on a decade longer, yielding its last trolley lines—the Church Avenue line and the McDonald Avenue line that it crisscrossed—to history on October 31, 1956.

Traces of trolley tracks can be found in parts of Manhattan and Brooklyn, anchoring parts of the city's past stubbornly in its present. At the Manhattan entrance to the Queensboro Bridge, an ornate trolley kiosk where passengers once boarded the yellow-and-orange trolleys that carried them over the East River, is looking for a home.

A plan to bring trolleys back to Forty-second Street floats above boardroom tables from time to time. In Brooklyn, plans to bring back trolley lines keep surfacing as well. Some, like the proposal to bring trolleys back to Red Hook's waterfront, have been dashed, while the recently organized Brooklyn City Streetcar Company's scheme may have a chance. The company has mapped out several lines, including one running through DUMBO (Down Under the Manhattan Bridge Overpass) and another along the waterfront area of Brooklyn Heights. Time will tell if these slow-moving charmers make a comeback or remain ghosts of another era.

SUBWAY STOPS ALONG

I love to pass those stations. They're all shadowy. Sometimes you see a figure, and you don't know if it's a transit worker or some homeless person who's made his shelter in that place. They have a kind of mystery and romance to them.

Ken Burns
documentary filmmaker

I loved the Redbirds that went out to Flushing. They weren't particularly attractive. I just associate them with a time in my life." Like many New Yorkers, Frank Buscaglia connects the deep-red IRT trains that plied the Flushing line in the 1980s with his adolescence, when he rode the Redbirds from Manhattan to his home in Bayside.

As with anything that weaves itself into our daily routine, the remembered look of a subway car can become an express trip back in time. "The old trains had straw seats, which were very durable," says William Bromberg, a former school administrator who grew up on the Upper West Side. "And I remember the straps. That's where the term 'straphanger' comes from." Subway cars with wicker seats, individual ceramic hand grips held by leather straps, big overhead fans, and vestibule entrances at either end of the car were, up until the 1960s, part of the subway experience. "I remember the fans," said Dennis Sidorick, another native New

THE WAY

PREVIOUS PAGES: A glimpse at the now abandoned platform of the Worth Street station that closed in 1962. Courtesy of A. Sumner-Sackett.

TOP LEFT: In the 1940s, porcelain handles and rattan seats greeted strap-hangers. TOP RIGHT: Subways are for working as this woman catches up on her typing. ABOVE: After World War II, trains had sleeker cars with fluorescent lighting and molded seats, although fans remained the only way to cool the cars. RIGHT: A subway ride from the Bronx to Manhattan gives these men time to catch up on baseball scores. All photographs from Photofest.

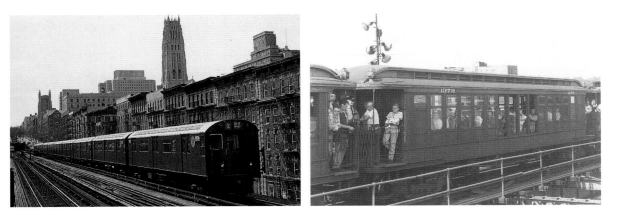

Yorker whose childhood in Manhattan involved a daily subway ride. "Someone next to me in a subway car was complaining about the lack of air-conditioning, and I had to tell him there was a time we never had air-conditioning. Just those big fans." Often during the summer months the doors connecting the cars were left open. "The windows and the doors between the cars would be open in the summer, and it got so noisy you couldn't carry on a conversation," says Frank Alexis, who as a young boy took the subway from his house in upper Manhattan to his midtown school.

Up until 1958, if you rode a BMT train along certain lines in the summer, you might be lucky enough to catch one of the convertibles providing its own form of air-conditioning. Removable panels on each car extending from the roof to just below the seat cushion ensured a brisk breeze as the train whisked along. By the 1970s, when subway cars were outfitted for real air-conditioning, the open front window was eliminated, a disappointment for many "junior" motormen like George Gildersleeve: "I would always try to get my father to ride in the first car so I could look out the window in the door next to the motorman's cab." The young Gildersleeve even made a study of which trains afforded the best view: "With the BMT Triplexes there was this inner door with only a very narrow window, more like a slot, that was very high up for a kid. The IND lines were much more accommodating, as there was a nice big window you could peer out and see exactly what the motorman saw."

ABOVE LEFT: A Redbird 2 train leaving the 125th Street station. This is the only outdoor section of the original line that opened on October 27, 1904. Photo by Eric Oszustowicz. ABOVE RIGHT: Subway fans take a farewell ride on a chartered train. The last open-gated elevated cars to run in New York City operated on the Myrtle Avenue el in 1958. From the collection of Steven Zabel, courtesy of Eric Oszustowicz.

If the IND and IRT trains had their admirers, it was those of the BMT that stole the show. Not only did they break the mold with their classic trains made up of the standard "sixty-seven-footers"—cars longer and wider than any of the IRT, with transverse seats and lots of windows—but the BMT line also boasted some of the best-looking trains. In 1934 the Zephyr, sporting lightweight stainless-steel cars with red leather upholstered seats, was introduced to straphangers along with the Green Hornet, named for the radio superhero. The Green Hornet, which ran across the same track line in Brooklyn where the infamous Malbone Street train wreck occurred, was an all-aluminum train painted a crisp two-tone green. Nicknamed "the Blimp" because of its wide sides, its doors closed to the sound of chimes. Lights were automatically turned on when a train entered a tunnel, and went out once the train was back in daylight. Unfortunately, the Green Hornet wasn't around for very long. With World War II came a demand for aluminum and, in 1942, one of the stars of the BMT's rolling stock was reduced to scrap metal.

On March 30, 1939, the Bluebird appeared, featuring cars with blue two-tone exteriors that resembled those of a luxurious long-distance train. The cars' interiors were done in soft blue, with mirrored paneling across the front and back sections and glare-free lighting. They were also articulated, with three sections linked together for a smoother ride. That technology wasn't new; articulated cars had been part of the BMT fleet as early as 1927 when the Triplex train, comprised of heavy cars with rattan seats, appeared and ran for almost forty years. But the Bluebird was remarkably eye-catching, and because the BMT had been able to place only a single five-car Bluebird on its tracks, its uniqueness added to its appeal. Why only one train? "The BMT ordered fifty more," says Donald Harold, founder of the Transit Museum. "But after the city took over the line, they were canceled and replaced by more heavyweight cars." Harold remembers catching the Bluebird on the Fourteenth Street–Canarsie line where it had become a great favorite. The Bluebird carried passengers over the Brooklyn Bridge to the Park Row terminal near City Hall until 1958, when it, too, was reduced to scrap metal.

If you ask New Yorkers of a certain age about the subway, many will remember it as an extension of home, and will recount a particular fondness for the subway lines they used. "Because I took the RR, which was the BMT's Fourth Avenue local from Brooklyn to Manhattan, that was the line I was most comfortable with," says Mary Michaelessi, a New Yorker who grew up in Brooklyn. "It gave me a real sense of Brooklyn because it stopped at all those wonderful streets: Union Street, Pacific Avenue, Atlantic Avenue."

"I remember feeling alienated whenever I went into the Eighth Avenue subway," says Dennis Sidorick who, as a child, usually took the IRT Seventh Avenue line from his Upper West Side apartment. "The platforms were wider, the seating arrangement on the trains was different. You got so used to riding one system that when you went to another you felt as if you were in another world."

Upstairs at street level, the IND station entrances were marked by simple green-and-white frosted globes, a far cry from the IRT's ornate kiosks that sheltered its station staircases. "Those kiosks were very nice, architecturally," says William Bromberg. "They had translucent glass and frames of copper which turned green, and fancy little roofs that reminded me of a Japanese pagoda." The kiosks not only shielded subway riders from the rain, they were a genteel reference point in the city, their elegant architecture inviting a civilized pause before one descended into the subway rush below. Then, upon exiting the horizontal world of the subway tunnel, one was immediately welcomed back into the vertical city.

Those whimsical reinterpretations of the Budapest summerhouses they copied have now vanished, along with trolley cars and the Third Avenue el. A replica of the IRT kiosk stands at Astor Place, a genuflection to a different time. Gone too are

OPPOSITE TOP: The BMT's Zephyr was the first stainless-steel car built for subway use. Its lightweight frame also made it available for elevated lines. Courtesy of A. Sumner-Sackett. OPPOSITE CENTER: Pullman also built the beautiful Green Hornet for the BMT. Like the Zephyr, its all-aluminum body was light enough for use on elevated lines. OPPOSITE BOTTOM: The BMT's Bluebird spent much of its career in service on the Canarsie line. This train is entering the Broadway Junction station. Center and bottom photos from the collection of Steven Zabel, courtesy of Eric Oszustowicz.

RIGHT: The Grand Central Shuttle's automatic canteen machines, October 1948. Courtesy of A. Sumner Sackett.
FAR RIGHT: Gene Kelly romances a picture of Vera-Ellen as "MissTurnstiles" in the 1949 musical film ON THE TOWN. Courtesy of Photofest.

the penny vending machines attached to subway-station pillars, which dispensed tiny packets of gum and candy. There were also round globes containing peanuts, banished supposedly because they were a great feasting place for mice. A story circulated that a woman's screams were heard up and down the platform one day after she had placed her hand under the peanut dispenser opening only to find a live mouse in it.

Another casualty of time was Miss Subways, a beauty contest that the IND launched in May 1941. "They got the idea from the Betty Grable pinup photos," says Ellen Strum, Miss Subways of March/April 1959. During the war years, one Miss Subways was pictured knitting a pair of argyle socks for her soldier boyfriend. The contest became so identified with the New York City subway, it was incorporated into *On the Town*, the Betty Comden–Adolph Green–Leonard Bernstein musical. In the movie version, sailor Gene Kelly catches a glimpse of the renamed Miss Turnstiles, played by dancer Vera-Ellen, and spends his twenty-four-hour leave in hot pursuit. In real life, Miss Subways became part of every straphanger's passing glance. "I'd take the Lexington Avenue train to 233rd Street and ride to work in Manhattan," says Arthur Michaelessi. "If I wasn't reading my *[New York] Daily Mirror*, I'd be gazing up at Miss Subways."

The contest ended in 1976, as much a victim of graffiti as it was of the changing times. While feminists demanded that contestants be addressed as "Ms.," tradi-

OPPOSITE: Mayor William O'Dwyer (center) drops a dime into the turnstile as part of the opening day ceremony for the IND Fulton Street branch in 1948. From the Brooklyn Public Library—Brooklyn Collection.

tionalists fretted that her image would become a canvas for vandalism. The contestants themselves objected to their inflated biographies and the meager prize: a silver charm bracelet boasting a subway token.

The changing of the guard is inevitable, even in a world hidden away twenty feet below the sidewalks. For anyone riding a subway in the 1940s, the cost of a subway ride was one nickel. Years after the subway system could no longer afford to sustain itself on the low revenue the price of a ride produced, that reliable nickel fare could not be touched. The frozen fare allowed New Yorkers to not only ride the subway to work, but to explore and experience their city. For people living in the outer boroughs, it meant an affordable trip to the city for dinner and a show. This was of course a time when inexpensive restaurant chains like the Automat and Schrafft's dotted Manhattan and the cost of a Broadway theater ticket was a few dollars. But that nickel fare was the key that unlocked the door to the grand metropolis.

Finally, on July 1, 1948, forty-three years after New Yorkers took their first subway ride, the price of the ride went up. Fares doubled on subway lines, making the cost of riding from the northern reaches of the Bronx to Brooklyn's Atlantic shoreline a whopping ten cents. To soften the blow, surface transportation went up a mere two cents. The ball was set in motion. Six years later, another nickel was added to the fare.

1953

1970

1988

1995

Since engineers felt it would be too difficult to redesign the turnstiles to accept two different coin denominations, the Transit Authority decided to mint a single token. On July 25, 1953, dime-size brass tokens—48 million of them—were minted, finding their way into the change purses and pockets of the city's straphangers. By 1970, when the fare rose to thirty cents, the small token with the familiar Y in the center was replaced by a slightly larger model. Ten years later, a third token style was manufactured, omitting the cut-out Y (part of the NYC logo). In

● ABOVE: Rattan seats and porcelain grippers are a thing of the past in today's subway cars. Courtesy of A. Sumner-Sockett.

1986, with the fare at one dollar, the bull's-eye token was introduced, which had a lead center. Then, in 1995, subway riders got their last token, one with a five-sided center aptly named the "five-borough." Today the MetroCard has replaced the token, relegating it to souvenir jewelry and keepsake boxes. For years the MetroCard had been under consideration. Not only does the card make fare increases an easier process, eliminating the need for new stock each time a new fare is introduced, it also simplifies the transfer process by eliminating paper tickets.

As time marched on, engineering advancements in the subways necessitated the closing of a handful of stations whose platforms were too short to accommodate longer, modern trains. A ride on the IRT—both the original Lexington Avenue route (4/6) and the one that runs up Broadway (1/9)—reveals the subway's past, as abandoned stations appear like ghosts, signposts to a time gone but not yet forgotten. The Eighteenth Street and the Worth Street stations, wedged between the Canal Street and Brooklyn Bridge stations, can be glimpsed while traveling on the local number 6 train or the express 4 or 5. The West Side's 1/9 trains take you past the graffiti-scarred Ninety-first Street station, a favorite of radio personality Jonathan Schwartz for whom it evokes pleasant memories: "It represents my childhood and a girl named Susan who lived on Ninetieth and Broadway," says Schwartz.

The centerpiece of the abandoned subway stops is the original City Hall station, August Belmont's 1904 masterpiece. To see the remnants of brass chandeliers and once-glistening stained-glass ceilings you must remain on the number 6 downtown local when it reaches the Brooklyn Bridge–City Hall station—its last stop—and travel with the train as it loops around the old station for the trip back uptown.

As for those old subway cars with their rattan seats, porcelain-and-leather straps, and overhead fans, they, too, are part of history, although a few have been salvaged and exhibited at the Brooklyn Transit Museum. In July 2003 the stripped-down shells of fifty Redbird cars were dumped in the Atlantic Ocean, about eight miles off

■ OPPOSITE: A barge filled with Redbirds on their way to Davy Jones' locker. Photo by Eric Oszustowicz.

Cape May, New Jersey. Later that year in October, the last of the Redbird cars was taken out of service. Like the nearly one thousand of their predecessors who have been sent to the ocean's bottom, the skeletal hulks will provide artificial reefs for fish and small plants. The one hundred remaining Redbirds will go to museums or be converted to work trains.

In the end, it is the subway experience itself that is rooted so deeply in the hearts and minds of New Yorkers. In his memoir, *New York in the '50s*, novelist and journalist Dan Wakefield writes of arriving in New York City from Indiana:

> *When New Yorkers said "train" it mean the subway. As in Duke Ellington's "Take the A Train," you took the train to go downtown to Greenwich Village or uptown to Columbia, on Morningside Heights. I took the IRT line to the local stop at 116th and Broadway and got off there to go to college. Crash and toot of congested traffic, underground earthquaking rush of the subway, faces black, yellow, and swarthy, voices speaking in foreign tongues, made the place seem as alien as Rangoon, yet I felt at home, sensing it was there I should be.*

Indeed, the subway was a rite of passage. For every straphanger newly arrived from Indiana, there was another subway rider who had traveled no farther than Brooklyn. As a young girl growing up in Brooklyn's Sunset Park, Mary Michaelessi discovered her future home because of the subway. "My mother would take us to the city on the subway to see Radio City Music Hall and the Rockefeller [Center] Christmas tree. As soon as I was able to ride the subway alone, I took it to Manhattan, got off on the Upper East Side, looked around, and said, 'This is where I'm going to spend the rest of my life.'" As a teenager, Michaelessi got her first taste of independence because of the subway. "As kids, my friend and I weren't allowed to do very much on our own, but we could take the subway to DeKalb Avenue to sample some of Junior's famous cheesecake. We would get off at the same subway stop to go to see Murray the K's rock 'n' roll show at the Brooklyn Fox." For Michaelessi, and for countless New Yorkers, native or newly arrived, the subway was the great emancipator, part of the road map to self-discovery. "The subway was a wonderful thing," Michaelessi says. "It still is."

TAKE ME OUT TO THE

Leave us make noise ●
for the boistrous boys
On the BMT.

"Leave Us Go Root for the Dodgers"
Dan Parker
NEW YORK DAILY MIRROR columnist

Ebbets Field was a narrow cockpit, built of brick and iron and concrete, alongside a steep cobblestone slope of Bedford Avenue. Two tiers of grandstands pressed the playing area from three sides, and in thousands of seats fans could hear a ball player's chatter, notice details of a ball player's gait and, at a time when television had not yet assaulted illusion with the Zoomar lens, you could actually see the actual expression on the actual face of an actual major leaguer as he played. You could know what he was like!

On the first page of his book *The Boys of Summer,* Roger Kahn describes not only the baseball stadium that was as much a part of Brooklyn as its famous bridge, but the romance and excitement of experiencing the Dodgers when they were the Brooklyn Dodgers, aka "Dem Bums," up close and personal. Ron Schweiger, who as a child of the fifties had only seen them on his black-and-white

BALLGAME!

TV, remembers his first game at Ebbets Field. "My father had box seats on the third-base side. As we walked up the ramp I saw my first glimpse of the field and stopped dead in my tracks. It was the greenest grass I had ever seen. I expected to see the game the way I had on TV, in black-and-white!"

Although they got their name from the trolleys that Brooklynites constantly dodged as they made their way to the ballpark, it was the subway that brought most of the fans to watch their home team. "We used to take the Brighton line," says Schweiger. "My mother would say to my brother and me, 'Remember, if you get the Brighton express it's three stops. If you get the local it's nine stops.'" To this day, New Yorkers speak of how, as their train left the tunnel and approached the station at Prospect Park—the Ebbets Field stop—the sight of sunlight gave them a jolt of excitement. "The trains were packed and it was hot," says George Gildersleeve. "But the fact that we were going to see the 'Bums' play made it all worthwhile." After getting off the train, folks walked through a wide corridor that led to Flatbush Avenue, where throngs of people getting off trolleys would join them. Three blocks away was the stadium that Charles Ebbets built.

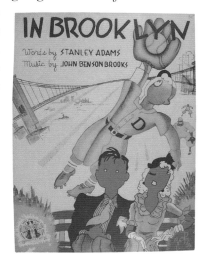

What would become the national pastime had made a giant footprint in Brooklyn, thanks to Ebbets. In 1911 the borough was losing most of its open fields to urbanization when former ticket-taker Charlie Ebbets went searching for land on which to build his stadium. One year later, he broke ground on a four-and-a-half-acre parcel along the eastern edge of Prospect Park, a former garbage pit nicknamed "Pigtown" by the natives, who brought their swine to the

fetid patch where they could feast on refuse. By the time Ebbets Field opened in 1913, the BRT, which already had streetcars and elevated trains in the borough, was about to become part of the new subway system. As people left the Lower East Side and crossed the East River to live here, an audience was building for the field in which the most democratic of sports was being played. "When people talk about the era of the Brooklyn Dodgers, they're talking about a period when the Jews and the Italians moved out of lower Manhattan into Brooklyn," says Barry Lewis. Many baseball players were the children of recent immigrants—uneducated, but talented and ambitious—who played out the American dream right there on the ball field, just a subway ride away.

In Brooklyn they had Ebbets Field, in Manhattan they had the Polo Grounds, and in the Bronx, Yankee Stadium. As early as June 28, 1911, when Ebbets was settling on land for his ball field, fans of the New York Giants could take August Belmont's seven-year-old IRT to 157th Street and walk a block east to Eighth Avenue where the new steel and concrete Polo Grounds rose, replacing an older stadium that had burned down just two months before. When the Eighth Avenue IND was completed, fans were practically in the ballpark when they arrived at their stop.

On April 18, 1923, just three blocks north of the Polo Grounds on the opposite

ABOVE LEFT: A pop-fly view of the IRT tracks and the Polo Grounds. From the collection of Andrew Grahl.
ABOVE RIGHT: The Lexington Avenue express at 161st Street and River Avenue. Courtesy of A. Sumner-Sackett.

OPPOSITE TOP: A Brooklyn trolley passing Ebbets Field. Print by Trolleyworks@AOL.com, courtesy of Joseph P. Saitta.
OPPOSITE BOTTOM: What could be more Brooklyn than a song that includes the Brooklyn Bridge and the Dodgers? Courtesy of the Larry Zimmerman Collection.

PREVIOUS PAGES: A Flushing-bound Redbird arrives at Shea Stadium. From the collection of Andrew Grahl.

RIGHT: Overview of Yankee Stadium (foreground) and the Polo Grounds separated by the Harlem River.
From the author's collection.

OPPOSITE TOP: Fans arriving at Yankee Stadium, 1953.
Courtesy of A. Sumner-Sackett.

OPPOSITE BOTTOM: "Ball Game Stop" beneath the track signal outside Yankee Stadium. © Bettman/CORBIS.

side of the Harlem River, the country's most famous baseball stadium was situated on what had been a patch of farmland. Dubbed the "House That Ruth Built" because it was said to have been designed in part to accommodate the hitting style of the great Babe Ruth, Yankee Stadium stretched from 157th to 161st Street and from River Avenue to Doughty Avenue. The triple-decked structure would become home to such "Bronx Bombers" as Lou Gehrig, Babe Ruth, Mickey Mantle, Roger Maris, Reggie Jackson, and, of course, Joe DiMaggio.

Dr. Edward J. Bottone remembers the subway ride that delivered him as a young boy to his hero: "I was a great fan of Joe DiMaggio. I would get on the first car of the Lexington Avenue IRT at 116th Street and look out the window. As the train ascended from the subway level aboveground, my heart would begin to pound. The train had a different sound as it began to make that climb." Some fans would sit on the left side of the subway car so that they could catch a glimpse of players at batting practice through the grandstand opening of the stadium. Bottone would often arrive at the end of the game, when he knew Joe DiMaggio was leaving: "You can't imagine the fantasy of a thirteen-year-old going to the stadium, knowing that at the end of the game you would see him. He'd come and sign my book. And then he would chase me home."

In the early days, before baseball players commanded million-dollar salaries, long before Major League baseball pitcher John Rocker made that infamous remark about the kind of people who ride New York City subways, baseball players regularly took the subway to their stadium. In Brooklyn, Bay Ridge was home to Duke Snider, Tommy Holmes, Rube Walker, Carl Erskine, and Pee Wee

Reese. Jackie Robinson, the first Dodger to break the color barrier, lived on Snyder Avenue in East Flatbush. Giants players lived at the Somerset Hotel on Seventy-second Street and Columbus Avenue or the Braddock at 126th Street and Eighth Avenue, and many of the Yankee players lived along the Bronx's Grand Concourse.

While the subways delivered the players safely to their stadiums, they also kept the streets clear for budding Babe Ruths to play stickball and stoopball. Peter Golenbock remembers those days in his book *Bums: An Oral History of the Brooklyn Dodgers:* "The streets had not yet been taken over by the automobile, because in Brooklyn there was a speedy and safe subway system that for five cents could take an explorer anywhere he wished to go in the borough and beyond."

In the 1950s, with the advent of television, came an even greater interest in baseball. Now fans could watch the game in their living rooms or at their favorite tavern. Pregame and postgame shows appeared on the air, creating new baseball celebrities. Actress Laraine Day, the wife of then Giants manager Leo Durocher, hosted a pregame show called *A Day in the Life of the Giants.* Baseball became the sound of summer as radios and TVs saturated the city with the voices of Mel Allen and Red Barber responding to that anticipated crack of the ball making contact with a bat.

Baseball games became a rite of passage from father to son, and the best way to get to the stadiums was by subway. "Everybody seemed to ride the subways," says former *New York Mirror* writer Arthur Richman in Harvey Frommer's *New York City Baseball: The Last Golden Age, 1947–1957.*

"There were kids with Giant caps, with Dodger caps, with Yankee caps, people with brown bags with their lunch going to games." As Frommer says, "Subways were for arguing about the New York City baseball teams, for anticipating what would happen at a game, for reviewing what had happened." And when the Yankees played the Dodgers or the Giants in a World Series, ushering in New York's Subway Series, the subway became a raucous traveling stadium.

As more New Yorkers migrated to the suburbs, beyond the subway's reach, cars replaced the trains as a means to reach stadiums. Since Ebbets Field had room for only seven hundred cars, parking presented a major problem. But there was another, more serious concern plaguing local baseball: City neighborhoods, including the one surrounding Ebbets Field, began to deteriorate in the wake of the middle-class exodus. The few cars coming to the park were vandalized, but worse yet, fans—especially women, who made up 30 percent of a game's attendance—began to feel unsafe. "I was very much concerned about the future when my mother-in-law and my wife wouldn't go to Ebbets Field because of the hoodlums and purse snatchers," said Dodgers president Walter O'Malley. The writing was on the wall: Ebbets Field was about to become history.

For a while, O'Malley flirted with another Brooklyn site at the intersection of Atlantic and Flatbush avenues. Not only did the Long Island Railroad arrive there, it was the only site in the city where three subway lines converged. Parks Commissioner Robert Moses gave that proposal the thumbs-down, arguing that it would be too costly. In the end, the lure of California proved too great for the president, and on October 8, 1957, Brooklyn lost its baseball team. This would be an especially bittersweet year for Brooklynites, whose cherished team had won their first World Series two years earlier. Meanwhile, the Giants were experiencing the same problem. "We never went to the Polo Grounds. It was too dangerous," says Tom Begner, who grew up in Manhattan in the 1950s. "Word had it that they couldn't fill the high-end seats anymore."

By the fall of 1957, the Giants followed the Dodgers to California, leaving New Yorkers without a National League baseball team, and with a very sour taste in their mouths. That same year, Mayor Robert F. Wagner announced that there would be

OPPOSITE: These SUBWAY SUN posters appeared above the doors in subway cars during baseball season to promote ridership to the games. Courtesy of A. Sumner-Sackett.

BELOW: All of Brooklyn wept when the Dodgers left Brooklyn. Courtesy of the Brooklyn Historical Society.

KEEP THE
Dodgers
IN BROOKLYN

another National League team in New York City: the Mets. Their stadium was built in Flushing Meadows on the site of the 1939 World's Fair—a few steps away from the IRT Flushing line, a location that had been proposed by Robert Moses and rejected by O'Malley in 1957 as an alternative stadium site for the Dodgers. O'Malley felt that once the Dodgers left Brooklyn they would no longer be the Brooklyn Dodgers, so he might as well negotiate for the best alternative site.

By 1960 the wrecker's ball had demolished Ebbets Field. Four years later, on April 10, 1964, that same wrecker's ball, its surface painted over with baseball scenes, was used to bring down the Polo Grounds. In 1972 Yankee Stadium underwent a four-year renovation, and while the stadium was being rebuilt, the Yankees played their '74 and '75 seasons at Shea Stadium alongside the Mets. There had been talk, when Rudolph Giuliani was mayor, of moving the Yankees to Manhattan, to a stadium that would be built on West Thirtieth Street near the Hudson River. That never happened, and although nothing is forever, the Yankees remain in the Bronx and the Mets are in Queens. For New Yorkers, both teams are just a subway ride away.

In spite of the fact that large numbers of seats are filled with fans who have arrived here by car from the suburbs, baseball in New York City continues to wear the street-smart edginess of its origins. Ride the Flushing IRT when a Mets game is about to start or the 4 train to Yankee Stadium when the Bronx Bombers are playing, and you'll come to believe that there are no cars or suburbs, just the city's baseball teams waiting for those subway cars to deliver the faithful.

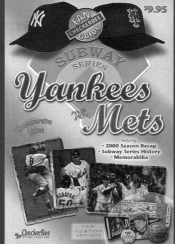

ABOVE: October 21, 2000—fans en route to Yankee Stadium for Game One of the World Series between the Yankees and the Mets. © Reuters/CORBIS. ABOVE RIGHT: Subway Series memorabilia. From the author's collection. RIGHT: Are they rooting for the Mets or the Yankees? Governor George Pataki, Senate candidate Rick Lazio, and Mayor Rudy Guiliani disembarking from the 7 train at Shea Stadium for Game Three of the World Series on October 24, 2000. © Reuters/CORBIS.

OPPOSITE TOP: Future batters and pitchers staring longingly at the House That Ruth Built. © Bettman/CORBIS. OPPOSITE BOTTOM: Baseball fans leaving a 7 train for Shea Stadium to watch the Yankees play the Mets in Game Three of the World Series. © Reuters/CORBIS.

THE RISE AND FALL AND RISE

Why do I continue to ride the subways? Even the
police now say they are too dangerous for a cop to
patrol without a companion cop to protect his back.

Russell Baker
NEW YORK TIMES, 1978

f you want to know anything about New York City,
about how its citizens are coping with life in their metropolis, you'll have to ride the subway. Down below the
streets of the city, you'll get an instant, accurate reading
of how New York City is doing. When former *New York
Times* columnist Russell Baker compared his daily descent
into the subway to a "torero confronting the bull," he was
writing about the out-of-control time in the 1970s when
youth gangs roamed the subways, seemingly impervious
to the efforts of the Transit Authority police to keep them
in check. Crime in the subways had gotten so bad, in 1979
it spawned a volunteer crime-fighting group calling itself
the Guardian Angels. Led by the charismatic Curtis Sliwa
and wearing red berets and T-shirts bearing the group's
logo, the young men and women of the Guardian Angels
became a strong presence, patrolling subway cars and
platforms, and occasionally making citizen's arrests.
What was happening in the subways was part of what was
happening all over the city.

AGAIN OF THE SUBWAY

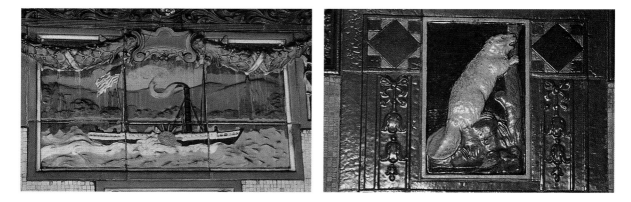

■ Decorative mosaics helped identify the neighborhoods above subway stations. Robert Fulton's steamship *Clermont* at Fulton Street (LEFT). The beaver that added to John Jacob Astor's wealth at Astor Place (RIGHT). OPPOSITE (CLOCKWISE FROM TOP LEFT): The vanished state prison at Christopher Street, St. John's Chapel at Canal Street, City Hall, Clark Street/Brooklyn Heights, and Borough Hall. Subway mosaic photography by Jim Melanson.

● PREVIOUS PAGES: Passengers on the 6 train had to contend with grafffiti-covered cars, a common sight in the 1970s. Copyright © 2000 by Robert Beckhard.

Back in 1904, the city that welcomed the first subway was solvent and optimistic. The new system carried New Yorkers into the twentieth century and even had a dash of glamour. It was important that the cars and the stations along the way be modern, attractive, and uplifting. After all, this transportation marvel, for all of its speed and convenience, was operating belowground, and people needed to be assured that they were entering an environment that was safe, clean, and comfortable. When architects George C. Heins and Christopher LaFarge, together with the Grueby Faience Company of Boston, were commissioned to design the mosaics and plaques for each of the IRT stations, their work had to serve a double purpose: They had to decorate the stations with lovely artwork keyed to the neighborhood, and whenever possible, they had to help identify the stations with "word pictures" for the growing immigrant population who could not understand English. Although it took a bit of foreknowledge to recognize that the gnawing beaver adorning the Astor Place station's plaque represented the means to John Jacob Astor's early wealth, the ships at the Fulton Street and Columbus Circle stops clearly reflected the nautical successes of both Robert Fulton and Christopher Columbus. Some plaques afford a glimpse of the city's vanished history. The Canal Street mosaic depicts the spire of St. John's Chapel, rising above beautiful St. John's Park near the Hudson River. Both the park and the chapel were destroyed in 1918 and replaced by a new freight depot for Cornelius Vanderbilt's Hudson River Railroad.

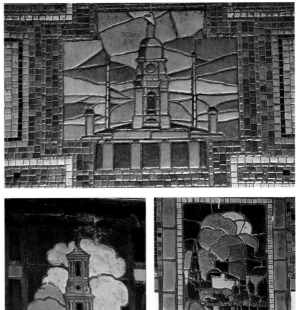

Gradually, those plaques that were once so eye-catching were made invisible by dirt and indifference. By the 1920s, the subway was simply an inexpensive, dependable means to get around the city. Unfortunately, the five-cent fare that made it widely accessible did nothing to help maintain the solvency of the system. Old subway cars got older and shabbier, and schedules were cut back. With New York City drowning in red ink, its subway system had to stretch every fare just to keep running.

With the Depression came a diminished tax base, drowning the already financially sinking system in red ink. Mayor Fiorello LaGuardia hoped that the city takeover of the lines in 1940 would consolidate and streamline the subway system. To some extent it did, but that five-cent fare was a killer. It was simply wildly unrealistic to expect a fare that came into existence in 1904 to remain frozen. By the time fares were raised in

1947, World War II was over and New Yorkers left the city in droves, searching for the American Dream in suburbia. As automobile assembly lines kicked into high gear, highways funded by the federal government were built. Those cars and those highways were taking the middle-class straphanger well beyond the reach of subways.

During the 1960s, the city's financial problems brought with them a crippling twelve-day transit strike. For nearly two weeks, the city and its inhabitants were frozen. Mary Michaelessi was a student when the strike occurred. "I lived in Bay Ridge and took two buses to school in Flatbush. Suddenly there were no buses. My father had to drive me to school. After classes were finished I had to stay at a friend's house until my father could pick me up hours later. It was a long walk to that friend's house." By the 1970s, New York City's money woes had deepened into a devastating fiscal crisis. If anyone had doubts that the city was in big trouble, one had only to ride a subway car. For, whatever it evolved into, when graffiti was scrawled across subway cars and station walls, it was not only a visual assault, it was testimony to a city descending into anarchy. Like a knife to flesh, it did not invite, it invaded. However sociologists choose to interpret or explain the need to "sign" on a public space, and however whimsical and colorful some of the scrawlings may have

been, they were given and received as an act of defiance, something that arose as much out of arrogance and anger as it did out of a need for a voice. In some cases, it was nothing more complicated than a way to fend off boredom or an audacious way of marking territory.

Before artists such as Keith Haring and Jean-Michel Basquiat declared it art and made it collectible, graffiti was one more sign of a city in deep trouble. It was also a reflection of a city out of control, of the helplessness its

Owen Smith, Artist

citizens felt as a result of the city's chronic insolvency. For anyone with a gripe and a spray can, the city and its subway system were theirs. In 1971 the Transit Authority spent $800,000 to remove graffiti from its subway cars and stations. The next year the graffiti budget rose to $1.3 million. No subway line was spared. It became a kind of game, as the graffiti artists found new ways to defeat the TA's attempts to clean up the vandalism. And after a while, it became part of counterculture chic. Although it wasn't surprising that pop artist Andy Warhol loved the scrawled-over cars, when Pulitzer Prize–winning author Norman Mailer wrote a book about it *(The Faith of Graffiti)*, it was clear that graffiti had become not only the new art form but a statement of the times.

As the city began to pull itself out of its financial hole, it reclaimed its status as the irresistible Big Apple. Attention was being paid to the world beneath the city streets and the subway system underwent a buffing up. In 1985, the MTA began the ambitious Arts for Transit program. Established artists such as Owen Smith, Ralph Fasanella, Faith Ringgold, and Mark Gibian were commissioned to transform subway stations into art galleries and themed environments—as Heins and LaFarge had done—corresponding to the neighborhoods aboveground.

At the Brooklyn Bridge–City Hall station, sculptor Mark Gibian has created a ceiling piece of cables beneath a skylight, evoking the cables on the famous bridge that the stop is partially named for. Faith Ringgold's historic Harlem figures done in ceramics float along the subway wall at the IRT's 125th Street stop, as if they had just drifted down from the street. Nowhere has a subway station been transformed more enchantingly than at the IND's Eighty-first Street station. Located

ABOVE: Owen Smith's "An Underground Movement: Designers, Builders, Riders" at the N/R's Sunset Park station in Brooklyn. Located at 36th St., M/N/R/W lines, commissioned and owned by the MTA Arts for Transit, 1998.

OPPOSITE TOP: Graffiti artist Keith Haring uses the subway station walls as his canvas. Haring helped turn graffiti into a collectible art. Keith Haring artwork © The Estate of Keith Haring.

OPPOSITE BOTTOM: Some graffiti could be quite whimsical, as seen on this subway car captured in a scene from Manfred Kirchheimer's film about graffiti-covered trains entitled STATIONS OF THE ELEVATED. Photofest.

beneath the American Museum of Natural History and the Rose Center for Earth and Space, this once-drab station is now a wonderland. A galaxy of stars and planets occupies one entrance, while a subterranean world of fish and sea creatures inhabits the other. At Times Square, artists Jacob Lawrence and Roy Lichtenstein have created vivid murals reflecting the vitality of the area. And at the Fourteenth Street station, Tom Otterness has brought whimsy to the area with his playful bronze pieces. Among them is an alligator rising from a city sewer. "We will be creating a new design aesthetic for this century as new stations are built, one that will hold up equally well with the older ones," says Sandra Bloodworth, director of Arts for Transit.

The days of dilapidated, graffiti-scarred subway cars are gone. Replacing the old rattling Redbirds are new sleek trains that are quieter, have air-bag suspension, ergonomically curved seats, and programmed messages recorded by dulcet-toned professionals to announce the stations. Cars are warm in winter and air-conditioned in summer.

And once again, the Second Avenue subway plans have resurfaced. If all goes according to plan, by 2016 New Yorkers will have a new East Side subway line run-

ABOVE: Roy Lichtenstein's "Times Square Mural" illustrates how artists have interpreted the neighborhoods above. RIGHT: Playful sea creatures at 81st Street beneath the American Museum of Natural History. Roy Lichtenstein's "Times Square Mural," designed 1990, fabricated 1994, installed 2002. Commissioned and owned by the MTA Arts for Transit. "For Want of a Nail," owned by MTA New York City Transit and commissioned by MTA in cooperation with the American Museum of Natural History.

OPPOSITE: This newly designed 6 train (Model R142A) will soon be a familiar fixture on the Lexington Avenue line. Designed by: Masamichi Udagawa and Sigi Moeslinger of Antenna Design, New York, in collaboration with Sandra Bloodworth, MTA Arts for Transit. Manufacturer: Kawasaki Rail Car. Photography: Ryuzo Masunaga.

ning from 125th Street to Hanover Square at Manhattan's southern tip, with sixteen subway stops along the way. As for the rest of the subway system, if Russell Baker is still riding it, he is likely finding that for all of its problems, it's not such a bad place after all. In fact, like most New Yorkers, he may decide it's the best ride in town.

To appreciate the impact of the subway on the lives of most New Yorkers, close your eyes and imagine the city without it. Better still, pick up a 1966 newspaper during the first days of the New Year when the city was paralyzed by its first transit strike, and picture yourself in those crowds of people trying to figure out how to get to and from work.

They may not be as quiet as Paris's Metro, as well-marked as London's Underground, or as museum-quality beautiful as Moscow's Metro, but where else can you ride 722 miles, twenty-four hours a day, seven days a week, from the Grand Concourse to Canarsie for a single fare? It's had its ups and downs to be sure, but anything in this city that is one hundred years old and still moving deserves a moment's pause. When New Yorkers descended the first set of subway stairs, farmland still existed above Forty-second Street. It was the subway that connected boroughs and created neighborhoods, putting the cap on Times Square as the entertainment mecca of the world and turning the Upper West Side into a thriving upper-middle-class community. Not only has the subway survived its bumpier rides, it remains the fastest way to get around, good enough to deliver, each morning, the city's 112th mayor to City Hall.

EPILOGUE

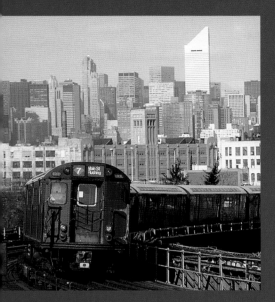

I could not have written this story without the resources of those subway mavens whose books on the New York City subway have turned what could have been a bumpy road into a smooth highway. Clifton Hood, Brian J. Cudahy, Stan Fischler, Benson Bobrick, Robert C. Reed, Robert Daly, and Peter Derrick are some of those writers. Thanks to Daniel Karatzas, whose book on Jackson Heights and generous assistance illuminated the once bucolic borough of Queens. Individuals who know the subway system far better than I very kindly shared their knowledge. A very special thanks to Don Harold, founder of the Transit Museum and true archivist of the subway system, who has become a good friend, and to Joe Cunningham, who painstakingly went over my text for accuracy. Larry Furlong shared his myriad contacts with me, putting me in touch with Andy Grahl and Eric Oszustowicz, both of whom turned over their priceless subway photograph collections. No one was more generous than Lawrence Stelter, who allowed me to use his father's beautiful photographs of the Third Avenue el. Jim Melanson helped illuminate the chapter on subway art with his lovely images of subway murals. How poor this book would have been without the stories of Barry Lewis, Larry Karlin, Jonathan Schwartz, Jimmy Skellas, Mary Michaelessi, Artie Michaelessi, Frank Alexis, Dr. Edward Bottone, Ron Schweiger, George Gildersleeve, Dennis Sidoric, and so many others. It was given added luster by my husband, Bill, who never fails to send the stars to me. I must thank my editors, Chris Pavone and Jennifer DeFilippi, who guided the book from conception to birth. Lastly, a very special thanks to my friend, Marianne Hardart, who took on the enormous task of finding the wonderful photos that have brought my text to life.

ACKNOWLEDGMENTS

Page 9: "like a sailboat before the wind" "Rapid Transit in New York," *Appleton's Journal:* 395. **Page 11:** "I won't pay political blackmail. . ." Robert Daley, *The World Beneath the City* (Philadelphia: J. B. Lippincott Co., 1959), p. 75. **Page 11:** "We propose to run the line to Central Park, . . . ibid, pp. 67–68. **Page 12:** "Night after night, gangs of men . . ." ibid, p. 67. **Page 13:** "Aladdin's cave." *New York Herald,* February 27, 1870. **Page 13:** "Under Broadway Reception." *New York Herald,* February 27, 1870. **Page 13:** "elegant reception room, the light, airy tunnel, and the general appearance of taste and comfort in all the apartments." *New York Times,* February 27, 1870. **Page 18:** "At Broadway near Trinity Church . . ." Robert C. Reed, *The New York Elevated* (South Brunswick and New York: A. S. Barnes and Company, 1978): p. 16. **Page 21:** "as rough as [riding in] an old-fashioned country wagon" James D. McCabe, Jr., *Lights and Shadows of New York Life* (New York: Farrar, Straus and Giroux, 1970): p. 216. **Page 21:** "lose his sense of smell . . ." Robert C. Reed, *The New York Elevated* (South Brunswick and New York: A. S. Barnes and Company, 1978): p. 20. **Page 21:** "We can travel from New York half-way to Philadelphia . . ." *New York Tribune,* June 6, 1878. **Page 21:** "companies sprang up in second-floor offices . . ." Robert C. Reed, *The New York Elevated* (South Brunswick and New York: A. S. Barnes and Company, 1978): p. 27. **Page 26:** "The ladies were evidently charmed . . ." *New York Herald,* June 6, 1878. **Page 30:** "Twenty great 'flag bombs' blasted into flight . . ." Benson Bobrick, *Labyrinths of Iron: Subways in History, Myth, Art, Technology, and War* (New York: Henry Holt and Company, 1994): p. 227. **Page 33:** "thought of the subway as a mission rather than a mere job" Clifton Hood, *722 Miles: The Building of the Subways and How They Transformed New York* (New York: Simon & Schuster, 1993): p. 79. **Page 33:** "Huge Mastodon bones were unearthed . . ." Benson Bobrick, *Labrynths of Iron: Subways in History, Myth, Art, Technology, and War* (New York: Henry Holt and Company, 1981): p. 230. **Page 39:** "We are here today for the purpose of . . ." Robert Daley, *The World Beneath the City* (Philadelphia and New York: J. B. Lippincott Company, 1959): p. 98. **Page 39:** "I now, as Mayor . . ." Robert Daley, *The World Beneath the City* (Philadelphia and New York: J. B. Lippincott Company, 1959): p. 99. **Page 40:** "cool little vaulted city of cream and green . . ." Benson Bobrick, *Labyrinths of Iron: Subways in History, Myth, Art, Technology, and War* (New York: Henry Holt and Company, 1994): p. 263. **Page 43:** "the night took on a carnival atmosphere . . ." Clifton Hood, *722 Miles: The Building of the Subways and How They Transformed New York* (Baltimore and London: The Johns Hopkins University Press, 1993): p. 95. **Page 45:** "complete with platforms, stairways, ticket booths . . ." Benson Bobrick, *Labyrinths of Iron: Subways in History, Myth, Art, Technology, and War* (New York: Henry Holt and Company, 1994): p. 263. **Page 47:** "little more than a geographical expression" Clifton Hood, *722 Miles: The Building of the Subways and How They Transformed New York* (Baltimore and London: The Johns Hopkins University Press, 1993): p. 101. **Page 47:** "sons of the mightiest metropolis . . ." Clifton Hood, *722 Miles: The Building of the Subways and How They Transformed New York* (Baltimore and London: The Johns Hopkins University Press, 1993): p. 101. **Page 57:** "It was from the El . . ." Alfred Kazin, *A Walker in the City* (New York: MJF Books, 1951): p. 137. **Page 59:** "barns and bee hives, carriage-houses and corn cribs" Daniel Karatzas, *Jackson Heights: A Garden in the City* (Grant from J. M. Kaplan Fund and the support of the Jackson Heights Beautification Group, 1990): p. 4. **Page 69–70:** "an avenue of expansion, connecting, in the process . . ." Ric Burns and James Sanders, with Lisa Ades, *New York: An Illustrated History* (New York: Alfred A. Knopf, 1999): p. 504. **Page 73:** "a grubby collection of four- and five-story brick tenements . . ." Clifton Hood, *722 Miles: The Building of the Subways and How They Transformed New York* (Baltimore and London: The Johns Hopkins University Press, 1993):, p. 210. **Page 76:** "one of the greatest engineering feats . . ." Groff Conklin, *All About Subways* (TK) **Page 76:** "I rode in the first city subway . . ." *New York Times,* December 15, 1940. **Page 76:** "I now formally open the Sixth Avenue subway . . ." *New York Times,* December 15, 1940. **Page 76:** "For last Christmas he gave us 'No El, No El' . . ." *New York Times,* December 16, 1940. **Page 77:** "Long, broad and brilliantly lighted" *New York Times,* December 16, 1940. **Page 82–83:** "The old mangy tenements . . ." Cornell Woolrich, *Death in the Air,* (*Nightwebs*) (Great Britain: Orion Books/The Orion Publishing Group, 2002): p. 226. **Page 86:** "I saw you,' said Step . . ." Cornell Woolrich, *Death in the Air (Nightwebs)* (Great Britain: Orion Books/The Orion Publishing Group, 2002): p. 243. **Page 86:** "incredibly rich and inviting . . ." Robert C. Reed, *The New York Elevated* (South Brunswick and New York: A. S. Barnes and Company, 1978): p. 99. **Page 87:** "The Third Avenue line carried gentry as well as poor folk . . ." Meyer Berger, *Meyer Berger's New York* (New York: Random House, 1953): p. 157. **Page 90:** "He took a street car . . ." Cornell Woolrich, *Dusk to Dawn (Nightwebs)* (Great Britain: Orion Books/The Orion Publishing Group, 2002): p. 198. **Page 92:** "For a trifling expense . . ." Henry Collins Brown, *In the Golden Nineties* (New York: Books for Libraries Press, 1970): p. 57. **Page 105:** "When New Yorkers said 'train' it meant . . ." Dan Wakefield, *New York in the Fifties,* Boston, New York, London: Houghton Mifflin/Seymour Lawrence, 1992): p. 24. **Page 107:** "Ebbets Field was a narrow cockpit, built of . . ." Roger Kahn, *The Boys of Summer* (New York: Harper & Row Publishers, 1971): pp. xi–xii. **Page 112:** "The streets had not yet been taken over . . ." Peter Golenbock, *Bums: An Oral History of the Brooklyn Dodgers* (New York: G. P. Putnam's Sons, 1984): p. 2. **Page 112:** "Everybody seemed to ride the subways . . ." (Arthur Richman) Harvey Frommer, *New York Baseball: The Last Golden Age, 1947–1957* (New York: Atheneum, 1985): p. 48. **Page 113:** "Subways were for arguing . . ." (Arthur Richman) Harvey Frommer, *New York Baseball: The Last Golden Age, 1947–1957* (New York: Atheneum, 1985): p. 48. **Page 113:** "I was very much concerned . . ." Harvey Frommer, *New York Baseball: The last Golden Age, 1947–1957* (New York: Atheneum, 1985): p. 3.

Berger, Meyer, *Meyer Berger's New York* (New York: Random House, 1953).

Bobrick, Benson, *Labyrinths of Iron: Subways in History, Myth, Art, Technology, and War* (New York: Henry Holt and Company, 1994).

Brooks, Michael W., *Subway City* (New Jersey and London: Rutgers University Press, 1997).

Brown, Henry Collins, *In the Golden Nineties* (New York: Books for Libraries Press, 1970). Note: First published in 1927: Valentine's Manual Number Twelve.

Burns, Ric, and James Sanders, *New York: An Illustrated History* (New York: Alfred A. Knopf, 1999).

Burrows, Edwin G., and Mike Wallace, *Gotham: A History of New York City to 1898* (New York: Oxford University Press, 1999).

Cudahy, Brian J., *How We Got to Coney Island: The Development of Mass Transportation in Brooklyn and Kings County* (New York: Fordham University Press, 2002).

———, *Under the Sidewalks of New York* (New York: The Penguin Group, 1979).

Daley, Robert, *The World Beneath the City* (Philadelphia and New York: J. B. Lippincott Company, 1959).

Derrick, Peter, *Tunneling to the Future: The Story of the Great Subway Expansion That Saved New York* (New York: New York University Press, 2001). Note: Copyright by The History of New York City Project, Inc..

Dreiser, Theodore, *Sister Carrie* (New York: The Modern Library, 1927).

Dwyer, Jim, *Subway Lives* (New York: Crown Publishers, Inc., 1991).

Ellis, Edward Robb, *The Epic of New York City: A Narrative History* (New York: Old Town Books, 1966).

Fischler, Stan, *Confessions of a Trolley Dodger* (New York: H & M Productions 11, Inc., 1995).

———, *Uptown, Downtown* (New York: Hawthorn Books, Inc., 1976).

Frattini, Dave, *The Underground Guide to New York City Subways* (New York: St. Martin's/Griffin, 2000).

Frommer, Harvey, *New York City Baseball: The Last Golden Age, 1947–1957* (New York: Atheneum, 1985).

Golenbock, Peter, *Bums: An Oral History of the Brooklyn Dodgers* (New York: G. P. Putnam's Sons, 1984).

Hjortsberg, William, *Falling Angel* (New York and London: Harcourt Brace Jovanovich, 1978).

Hood, Clifton, *722 Miles* (New York: Simon & Schuster, 1993).

Immerso, Michael, *Coney Island: The People's Playground* (New Brunswick, New Jersey, and London: Rutgers University Press, 2002).

Kahn, Roger, *The Boys of Summer* (New York: Harper & Row Publishers, 1971).

Karatzas, Daniel, *Jackson Heights: A Garden in the City* (Grant from J. M. Kaplan Fund and the support of the Jackson Heights Beautification Group, 1990).

Kazin, Alfred, *A Walker in the City* (New York: MJF Books, 1951).

Kramer, Frederick A., *Across New York by Trolley* (New York: Quadrant Press, Inc., 1975).

———, *Building the Independent Subway: The Technology and Intense Struggle of New York City's Most Gigantic Venture* (New York: Quadrant Press, Inc., 1990).

Lavis, Fred, *Building the New Rapid Transit System of New York City Circa 1915* (Originally reprinted from *Engineering News*, 1915, and reproduced by Xplorer Press, New Jersey, 1996).

Love, Edmund G., *Subways Are for Sleeping* (New York: Harcourt, Brace and Company, 1956).

McCabe, James D., Jr., *Lights and Shadows of New York Life* (New York: Farrar, Straus and Giroux, 1970).

McCullough, David, *The Great Bridge: The Epic Story of the Building of the Brooklyn Bridge* (New York: Simon & Schuster, 1972).

Miller, John Anderson, *Fares, Please!: A Popular History of Trolleys, Horsecars, Streetcars, Buses, Elevateds, and Subways* (New York: Dover Publications, Inc., 1941).

New York Interborough Rapid Transit Company, *Interborough Rapid Transit: The New York Subway, Its Construction and Equipment* (New York: Arno Press, 1904).

New York Railways: The Green Line (New York: N.J. International, Inc., 1994).

Queen, Ellery, *Cat of Many Tails* (Boston: Little, Brown and Company, 1939).

Range, Tom, Sr., *Postcard History Series: New York City Subways* (South Carolina: Arcadia Publishing, 2002).

Reed, Robert C., *The New York Elevated* (South Brunswick and New York: A. S. Barnes and Company; London: Thomas Yoseloff Ltd., 1978).

Royster, Vermont, *My Own, My Country's Time* (North Carolina: Chapel Books, 1983).

Salwen, Peter, *Upper West Side Story: A History and Guide* (New York: Abbeyville Press, Inc., 1989).

Sansone, Gene, *Evolution of the New York City Subways: An Illustrated History of New York City's Transit Cars, 1867–1997* (Baltimore: The Johns Hopkins University Press, 1997).

Snyder-Grenier, Ellen M., for The Brooklyn Historical Society, *Brooklyn!: An Illustrated History* (Philadelphia: Temple University Press, 1996).

Spann, Edward K., *The New Metropolis: New York City, 1840, 1857* (New York: Columbia University Press, 1981).

Stelter, Lawrence, *By the El* (New York: H & M Productions, Inc., 1995).

Sullivan, Neil J., *The Dodgers Move West* (New York: Oxford University Press, 1987).

Tygiel, Jules, *Past Time: Baseball As History* (New York: Oxford University Press, 2000).

Wakefield, Dan, *New York in the Fifties* (Boston, New York, London: Houghton Mifflin/Seymour Lawrence, 1992).

Willensky, Elliot, *When Brooklyn Was the World* (New York: Harmony Books, 1986).

Woolrich, Cornell, *Death in the Air* (Great Britain: The Orion Publishing Group, 2002).

air quality issues, 45–46
archaeological finds, 33, 55

baseball stadiums, 107–14
Beach, Alfred Ely, 9–15
Bedford-Stuyvesant, 51, 70
Belmont, August, 31–32, 40,
    44–46, 52–54
Bluebird trains, 100–101
BMT (Brooklyn Manhattan
    Transit Corporation), 67,
    72–73, 77, 99–101
Brighton Beach, 65, 93–94
Bronx, 26, 65
Brooklyn, 26, 49–51, 54–55, 66
Brooklyn Bridge, 27, 37, 51
Brooklyn Dodgers, 93, 107–8, 113,
    114
Brooklyn Rapid Transit line,
    14–15
Brooklyn Transit Museum, 104
Brownsville, 49–51
BRT (Brooklyn Rapid Transit
    Company), 51, 54–57, 61,
    66–67

Coney Island, 65–66, 94

Ebbets Field, 107–9, 113, 114
Eighth Avenue line, 70–71, 76
elevated railways
    Brooklyn Elevated Railroad, 27
    dismantling of, 78–79
    first built, 22–23
    Fulton Street el, 51, 78
    Gilbert elevated, 25–26
    Greenwich Street, 23
    Manhattan Elevated, 26
    Metropolitan Railway, 26
    New York Elevated Railway,
        24–25, 26
    Ninth Avenue el, 78
    Second Avenue el, 78
    Sixth Avenue el, 73, 76–77
    Third Avenue el, 78, 81–87

fares, subway, 65, 67, 103–4, 120
Fasanella, Ralph, 121

Flushing Line, 61, 67
Fulton Street elevated, 51, 78

Garden City community, 62
Gibian, Mark, 121, 122
Gilbert, Rufus, 21–22, 25
Gilbert elevated, 25–26
Giuliani, Rudolph, 114
graffiti, 120–21
Green, Andrew Haskell, 26
Green Hornet trains, 100
Greenwich Street elevated, 23
Grueby Faience Company, 118
Guardian Angels, 117
Guastavino, Rafael, 40

Harlem, 64, 69–71
Harvey, Charles T., 22
Hedley, Frank, 42–43
Heins, George C., 118
Heins & LaFarge, 40
horsecars, 20–21
Hudson & Manhattan Railroad
    Company, 37, 53
Hylan, John F., 67, 70

IND (Independent), 70, 72–73, 76,
    77, 101
Interborough-Metropolitan, 53, 54
IRT (Interborough Rapid Transit
    Company)
    competing subway lines, 56–57,
        72
    construction of, 30, 33–36
    creation of, 32
    financing of, 31–32
    kiosk entrances, 40, 101
    line extensions, 47, 55, 61, 67
    opening day ceremonies, 39–45
    ownership of, 77
    station artwork, 118
    subway cars, 46, 56, 97–98

Jackson Heights, 60, 62, 67

kiosk entrances, 40, 101

LaFarge, Christopher, 118

LaGuardia, Fiorello, 73, 76, 77,
    120
Lawrence, Jacob, 122
Lichtenstein, Roy, 122
Long Island Railroad, 61
The Lost Weekend (movie), 81, 86

MacDonald, John B., 31, 40
MacDougall, Edward Archibald,
    59–61, 62
Manhattan Elevated, 26
McAdoo, William, 53
McAneny, George, 54
McClellan, George B., 39–43, 76
MetroCards, 104
Metropolitan Street Railway, 26,
    53
Meyer, Cord, 60
Mineola (subway car), 46
Miss Subways, 102–3
Moses, Robert, 113, 114

Newtown, 60
New York City Transit System, 77
New York Elevated Railway,
    24–25, 26
New York Giants, 109, 113
New York & Harlem Railroad, 20
New York Mets, 114
New York Railways, 90, 95
Ninth Avenue el, 78

omnibuses, 20–21
On the Town (musical/movie), 102
Ottermess, Tom, 122

Parsons, William Barclay, 33, 34, 40
PATH (Port Authority Trans-
    Hudson), 37, 53
Payton, Philip A., Jr., 64
Pennsylvania Railroad, 37, 61
Pennsylvania Station, 37, 61
pneumatic tube, 10–15
population, New York City, 26–27
Public Service Commission (PSC),
    53

Queens, 26, 60–62

Rapid Transit Commission, 25, 33,
    52, 53
Redbird trains, 97, 104–5
Ringgold, Faith, 121, 122
Rockefeller, John D., 76
Rockefeller, Nelson, 79

Second Avenue el, 78
Second Avenue line, 78–79
Sixth Avenue el, 73, 76–77
Sixth Avenue line, 76
Smith, Owen, 121
Speedy (movie), 86
Standards (BRT cars), 56
"straphanger" definition, 97
streetcars, 89–95
subway cars, 56, 97–101, 104–5
subway stations, 40, 77, 101, 102,
    118–22
Sunnyside Yards, 61

Tammany Hall, 11, 30–31
Third Avenue el, 78, 81–87
Third Avenue Railway, 90, 95
tokens, 103–4
Trains Meadow, 59–60
transit strike, 120
Triborough System, 53
Triplex trains, 99
trolley cars, 89–95
Tweed, Boss, 11–12, 14, 30
12 Angry Men (movie), 86

Upper West Side, 24, 64

Van Wyck, Robert, 30

Wagner, Robert F., 113–14
Walker, Jimmy, 70–71
West Side and Yonkers Railway,
    22–23
Winters, Edwin W., 54
Woodside, 61

Yankee Stadium, 109, 111, 114

Zephyr trains, 100

INDEX

THE GUGGENHEIM
MEMORIAL CONCERTS-
THE GOLDMAN BAND

The Sub

Vol. XVII

BOARD OF

you, too, can

BEACH
EXPRESS

REA

by

co

PELH

OPPY